The Gunp

Terror & Faith in 1605

~

ANTONIA FRASER

Volume Two

History to the defeated
May say Alas but cannot help nor pardon –

W. H. AUDEN, Spain, 1937

PHOENIX

This edition produced for The Book People Ltd,
Hall Wood Avenue, Haydock, St Helens WA11 9UL

First published in Great Britain in 1996
by Weidenfeld & Nicolson Ltd
First published in paperback in 1997
by Mandarin Paperbacks

Paperback edition published in 2002
by Phoenix,
an imprint of Orion Books Ltd,
Orion House, 5 Upper St Martin's Lane,
London WC2H 9EA

A CIP catalogue record for this book is available from the British Library.

ISBN 978 1 4072 1614 0

Printed and bound in Great Britain by
Clays Ltd, St Ives plc

The Orion Publishing Group's policy is to use papers that are natural, renewable
and recyclable products and made from wood grown in sustainable forests. The
logging and manufacturing processed are expected to conform to the environmental
regulations of the country of origin.

www.orionbooks.co.uk

Contents

CHAPTER ELEVEN

Mr Fawkes Is Taken

~⌐

Catesby sent for me into the fields...So I went to
him, who told me that Mr Fawkes was taken and the
whole plot discovered.

CONFESSION OF ROBERT WINTOUR
1606

Salisbury put the Monteagle letter in front of his royal
master on Friday 1 November. The King had returned
from hunting the previous day, but Salisbury evidently felt
no need to quicken his pace and waited until the afternoon to
give it to him. The King was alone in his gallery at Whitehall.
Salisbury handed him the letter without comment and let the
King read it in silence. Having read the letter once, James took
'a little pause', then he re-read it all through.*[1]

Salisbury said that the letter must have been written 'by a fool'.
This was a deliberate ploy, Salisbury explained afterwards. He
wanted to be sure to get his master's true reaction. Salisbury drew
particular attention to the phrase 'the danger is passed as soon as
you have burnt the letter', which, he said, he found quite mean-
ingless. It was his sagacious master – so experienced in the ways
of conspiracies in both England and Scotland – who puzzled out
the answer. James believed that something to do with 'powder'
was being suggested – in other words an explosion.

* These and the following details are taken from King James' own account, published in the so-called King's Book (printed as King's History in S.T., II, pp.
195–202). We therefore have his point of view, but Salisbury's point of view, of
course, only in so far as he communicated it to the King.

At this point, one might have thought that Salisbury — a sincerely concerned Salisbury — would have dropped his pretence of bafflement. If he had been in genuine ignorance about the meaning of the anonymous letter, surely this was the occasion to reveal at the very least the intelligence reports he had been receiving over the past year about Catholic unrest. But still Salisbury thought it best to 'dissemble' to the King; he did not tell James that there was already 'just cause' for apprehension about the Catholics' future behaviour. The King's fine questing intellect was to be allowed to flourish in a vacuum; its triumph when it pointed brilliantly to the solution would be all the greater. This at least was the gist of Salisbury's explanation afterwards to the King.

One may suppose that the true explanation was rather different; Salisbury was still in the dark about many details of the Plot, especially about the involvement, if any, of the leading nobles. He wished to lead his master to discover it more or less single-handed (with a little help from Monteagle), but he did not wish to embroil him in the murkier details of Salisbury's counter-plotting. Above all, Salisbury had no wish to arouse in King James those ever lurking fears for his personal safety which might have led to him insisting on springing the trap too soon. Thus Salisbury carefully managed the elaborate ritual of his consultation with the King.

On this same Friday a very different kind of ritual was taking place in far-off Warwickshire. While Salisbury nonchalantly conversed with the King in Whitehall, the Feast of All Saints was being solemnly marked at Coughton Court. If the pilgrimage to St Winifred's can be seen as an elegy to the recusant way of life, so this festival at Coughton may be viewed with similar nostalgia as the last great celebration of the English Catholic world: a world which was essentially loyal despite harassment, peace-loving despite suffering, and, where persecution was concerned, submissive to the will of God. They were all of them, the priests, the gentlemen and the gentlewomen, the faithful servants, about to see this world blown apart.

Coughton Court was an appropriate setting for such a solemnity.[2] It had belonged to the Throckmortons since the early fifteenth century and had been extended in Elizabethan times into a spacious and beautiful house with its 'stately castle-like Gate-house of freestone', in the words of the seventeenth-century antiquary Dugdale. Coughton also commanded from its flat roofs amazing views of the surrounding countryside. This was a perspective which would be useful in perilous times of searches by eager poursuivants.

For the staunchly recusant Throckmortons, these perilous times had lasted since the Reformation. A Throckmorton cousin had been executed in 1584 for a plot to free Mary Queen of Scots. Thomas Throckmorton, the present head of the family, like his brothers-in-law Sir William Catesby and Sir Thomas Tresham, had been persistently fined and had spent many years in prison. It was hardly surprising that by 1605 Coughton's gracious structure had its secrets, including a hiding-place in the north-eastern turret of the so-called Tower Room, with its inner and outer compartments, which was most probably the work of Little John, and there may well have been others.*

At High Mass on All Saints' Day, in front of a great gathering of Catholics, Father Garnet preached a sermon on the theme of a Latin hymn from the Office of Lauds: 'Take away the perfidious people from the territory of the Faithful.' The government prosecutor, Sir Edward Coke, afterwards used this text to suggest that Garnet had 'openly' prayed for 'the good success' of the Powder Plot, four days before it was due to happen. Such a prayer supporting treason, declared Coke, counted far more than mere consent, which he suggested Garnet had also given. In fact Garnet's correspondence around this time provides ample evidence of a concern for Catholic

---

* When this hole was broken into in 1858, a palliasse bed, a rope ladder, a small piece of tapestry and a folding leather altar were discovered within. Coughton Court is today leased to the National Trust, although the direct Throckmorton descendants are still closely involved with it. Coughton is proud of its connection to the Gunpowder Plot: a special exhibition has been mounted to commemorate it.

suffering which would justify the use of such a text. In October he wrote to Rome to say that the persecution was now 'more severe than in [Queen] Bess' time', with the judges openly saying that 'the King will have blood'. He later explained publicly that the text referred to the prospect of 'sharper' anti-Catholic laws in the coming Parliament.*³

The next day, 2 November, the Coughton party turned to the more melancholy rituals of All Souls Day, feast of the dead. This protracted sojourn of the Digby household at Coughton – Lady Digby and her small sons, of whom the elder Kenelm was only two – did not however pass unremarked. Also on 2 November, Father John Gerard came over to Gayhurst from Harrowden (presumably to say Mass). He was disconcerted to find the household vanished, with only Sir Everard remaining, making visible preparations for his 'hunting party'. Father Gerard then had a long conversation with Digby in which he asked some searching questions. Was there 'any matter in hand'? And, if so, did 'Mr Whalley' (an alias for Garnet) know about it?

'In truth, I think he does not,' replied Digby. There was 'nothing in hand' that he, Digby, knew of, 'or could tell him of'. This was of course disingenuous, to put it mildly, since Digby had been assured of Jesuit approval of the treason less than a fortnight earlier. Digby's honourable intention was to protect Gerard from implication in the Plot, and in a sense he did so successfully since Gerard afterwards called the conversation to witness as proof of his innocence. But Father Gerard, who was extremely averse to such 'violent courses', would always regret that he had not had an opportunity to try to dissuade Digby from his dreadful purpose.⁴ So Digby was left to his own devices – or rather to those of his hero, Robin Catesby.

Saturday 2 November was also the day on which the

---

* Father Garnet has been called 'unwise' for using such a text (although it formed part of the Office of Lauds for that day): but it is likely that whatever text he used for a sermon so close to the chosen date of the Powder Treason would have been twisted in some way by the government (Anstruther, *Vaux*, p. 281).

Council resolved to take some action on the question of the threat to Parliament reported to them by Salisbury. Various Privy Councillors came to see the King in his gallery in his Whitehall palace. They told him that it had been decided that the Lord Chamberlain, Lord Suffolk, should 'view' the Houses of Parliament 'both above and below'. Yet, once again, urgency was scarcely the key-note of the proceedings. This expedition would not take place until the Monday, partly to prevent unlawful rumours spreading, and partly because it would be best to make the search 'the nearer that things were to readiness'.[5]

This decision, along the same lines as Salisbury's wish to let the Plot 'ripen', makes little sense if the Councillors were really in complete ignorance of what was being planned. By Saturday a full week had passed during which Salisbury and selected Councillors had been aware, thanks to the Monteagle Letter, that 'a terrible blow' might be struck at Parliament. To leave things as they stood for another forty-eight hours was recklessly irresponsible – unless Salisbury had taken his own steps to secure the safety of the building.

On Sunday evening, 3 November, Thomas Percy, back from the north, had a conference with Catesby and Wintour in London. By now Catesby and Wintour had been urged more than once by Francis Tresham to abandon their venture and flee because of the sinister omen of the Monteagle Letter. But Catesby would still have none of it. Percy, similarly resolute, declared himself ready to 'abide the uttermost trial'.[6]

It is possible that some rearrangement of the plans for a royal abduction was discussed at this late stage. There was a story afterwards about a visit to the young Prince Charles, Duke of York, by Percy: this at a time when everyone was trying to get in on the act (and please the government) by offering helpful information. According to the deposition of one Agnes Fortun, servant, Percy came to the little Duke's lodgings on or about 1 November and 'made many enquiries as to the way into his chamber', also 'where he rode abroad' and with how many attendants. But by the time this deposition was given it was too late for Percy to confirm or deny it. Wintour's version in his confession has the London conspirators getting word indirectly that Prince Henry was not after all going to the Opening of Parliament: which would have made the kidnapping of the second son pointless.[7] (This was hardly the line taken by the government subsequently. There were few references to the Powder Treason which did not drag in the fact that the royal heir – the kingdom's hope for the future – had been in the same appalling danger as his father.)

Events were now moving at such a pace that one cannot be absolutely certain what Catesby, Wintour and Percy discussed at this meeting. Guy Fawkes' statement that after 'sundry consultations' it was considered easier to abduct the Princess Elizabeth in the midlands rather than the Duke in London 'where we had not forces enough' remains, however, more convincing. (As for the fourth royal child, Princess Mary, aged six months, Guido admitted her kidnapping was discussed – but they 'knew not how to come by her'.) Sir Everard Digby's departure for Dunchurch, south of Rugby, the next day reinforces Fawkes' testimony. The point of Dunchurch, Digby stated later, was that it was only eight miles from where the Princess was housed at Coombe Abbey, so that she could be 'easily surprised'.[8]

Monday 4 November, therefore, saw Sir Everard Digby and seven servants installed at the Red Lion in Dunchurch, near Dunsmore Heath, where the 'hunting party' was to take place.* He travelled as the gallant he was, taking with him not only servants but a trunk of clothes which included 'a white satin doublet cut with purple' and other satin garments thickly encrusted with gold lace. Digby was joined by his uncle Sir Robert Digby and two Littletons, 'Red Humphrey' and his very tall, very dark nephew Stephen. These men were not conspirators but they were recusants or had recusant sympathies (Humphrey Littleton, like Thomas Habington, had been among those who had tried to get a Catholic MP elected locally in 1604).[9]

* The Red Lion at Dunchurch is now a private residence, known as Guy Fawkes House.

The whole party had a convivial supper at the inn. Later, a message was sent to John Wintour, step-brother of Robert and Tom from their father's second marriage, who happened to be at Rugby. He was invited to join them in order 'to be merry' together. Later still, John Grant and a friend, Henry Morgan, who had been sworn to secrecy at Grant's house, also joined them.[10] There was a Catholic priest in the party, Father Hammond, who said Mass early the next day, before the hunt moved off.

At eleven o'clock on the morning of Monday 4 November, Thomas Percy appeared at Syon House, the great house on the Thames, to the west of London, which belonged to his patron the Earl of Northumberland. This foray, which would bring about the downfall of Northumberland, was actually a fishing expedition on Percy's part. For all Catesby's bravado and Percy's own resolution, the Monteagle Letter could not be dismissed entirely. Percy decided to go down to Syon to find out what rumours, if any, had reached Northumberland (a member of the Privy Council). 'If ought be amiss,' he told Wintour and Catesby, 'I know they will stay [detain] me.' He used the excuse that he wanted a loan from Northumberland. Percy encountered his patron, talked to him, found to his great relief nothing out of the ordinary about his reception, and set off back to London about one o'clock.[11]

The timing of this visit was extraordinarily damaging to Northumberland. It was characteristic of the ruthless and self-centred Percy, a middle-aged man without any of the impetuosity forgivable to youth, that he did not seek to protect the man who had treated him so generously. He might at the very least have avoided Northumberland's company, but Percy did not even warn Northumberland to avoid Parliament next day, as his patron's subsequent moves demonstrate.

Afterwards Northumberland desperately tried to exculpate himself. Unfortunately he was in the position of a man who, all unawares, has had an encounter with a plague-carrier – and finds out too late to avoid suspicion of having caught the plague himself. He remembered the conversation in the hall at Syon, denied that it had had any treasonable content whatsoever, declared merely that Percy had asked him 'whether he would command any service' before going on his way. Yes, he had sent a message after Percy, but that was purely to do with the audits of the northern properties for which Percy collected the rents.[12]

What Northumberland did not know was that Thomas Percy on his return to London also paid a visit to Northumberland's London home, known as Essex House. There Percy saw his nephew Josceline, who was in the Earl's service.[13] No doubt Percy was also testing the waters at Essex House. But the double visit would ensnare Northumberland still further. As for Northumberland himself, he stayed at Syon till after dinner, when he sent for his horses to take him to London, where he would spend the night at Essex House. He had not applied for leave of absence from Parliament, and showed every sign of intending to go there – he had his servant bring up 'the necessaries for Parliament' from Syon – apart from one spasm of fatigue which passed.* Even the King, in a handwritten note directed to Salisbury, afterwards drew attention to the innocence of Northumberland's behaviour: 'as for his purpose of not going to Parliament, he only said at dinner that he was sleepy for [because of] his early rising that day, but soon after changed his mind and went.'[14]

About five or six o'clock in the evening, Thomas Percy assured Wintour, Jack Wright and Robert Keyes that 'all was well'. After that compromising visit to his nephew at Essex House, Percy went to his own lodging in the Gray's Inn Road, where he left orders for his four horses to be ready for an extremely early departure the next day. Late that night Robin Catesby set off for the midlands, to take part in the rising, the vital second stage of the Plot, and it seems that Jack Wright, his faithful henchman, and his servant Thomas Bates went

* There were ten bishops and forty peers eligible to sit in the House of Lords, of whom twenty-nine had appointed proxies; but Northumberland was not among them (Anstruther, 'Powder', p. 457).

with him as well. This public display of armed rebellion was intended to rally Catholics everywhere to the cause. At 10.00 p.m. Guido Fawkes visited Robert Keyes and was handed a watch which Percy had left for him to time the fuse. An hour later John Craddock, a cutler from the Strand, brought Ambrose Rookwood the finest of all the engraved swords with the words 'The Passion of Christ' upon them.

But Thomas Percy was quite wrong. All was not well. For the hunters who were themselves being hunted, the last stage of the chase was beginning.

Monday was also the day on which members of the Council, headed by Lord Suffolk as Lord Chamberlain, were due to make their long-delayed search of Parliament, 'both above and below'. The official story told afterwards was of two searches, with a visit to the omniscient King in between. Nevertheless, Salisbury's first report of these tumultuous events (to the English ambassadors abroad) mentioned only one search – and that around midnight. Salisbury, however, may have been at this point concerned to simplify, for the sake of foreign consumption, what was certainly a very elaborate tale.[15] What is quite clear is how the search (or searches) ended.

Accepting the King's version, Lord Suffolk made the first search on Monday, accompanied by among others Lord Monteagle, whom he sent for from Monteagle's house in the Strand. Suffolk deliberately conducted himself in the most casual manner possible. He took care not to arouse the suspicions of a tall man standing in or near the cellar who appeared to be some kind of servant. In the words of the King, Suffolk merely cast 'his careless and his rackless [reckless] eye' over the scene. But his eye was not so careless that it did not observe an enormous amount of firewood – piles of faggots – heaped up in the cellar. Yet the lodging it served was quite small.

That was one surprise. The second came when the party was told by John Whynniard, owner of the house, that his current tenant was none other than Thomas Percy, kinsman and employee of the Earl of Northumberland.[16] That made the unusual quantity of firewood even more astonishing, since

Percy was well known to have his own house elsewhere in London and seldom slept at Westminster. The news also provoked from Monteagle a histrionic flash of revelation. Surely Percy must be the author of the anonymous letter? Monteagle told Suffolk that, as soon as he heard the name, he knew Percy must be his man. There was not only Percy's 'backwardness' in religion, that is his Catholicism, which pointed to him, but there was also that 'old dearness of friendship' which Percy felt for Monteagle, to explain the warning.

Monteagle – and Salisbury – were of course bound to produce an author, or at least a suspected author, of the letter which they themselves had actually concocted. Percy's was a convenient name: as tenant of the cellar, there was no question about his involvement in the conspiracy (all the details of which were not yet revealed). But, for the members of the Privy Council not in the know, the name of Percy was somewhat of an embarrassment. On the one hand they were anxious to secure the safety of Parliament. On the other hand, the whole matter – anonymous letter and all – might be 'nothing but the evaporisation of an idle brain'. Percy's connection to Northumberland, 'one of his Majesty's greatest subjects and councillors', was well known. They would be 'loath and dainty [reluctant]' to interfere unnecessarily in such a way as to cast aspersions on such an august figure.

The King was not content with this dainty approach. When he heard what had taken place, he pointed out sensibly enough that either a proper search must be made, or he would 'plainly …go next day to Parliament' and leave the outcome of the day 'to fortune'. It seemed right that 'a small party' under Sir Thomas Knevett, a member of the King's Privy Chamber but also, conveniently, a Justice of the Peace for Westminster, should make a further discreet investigation.

Thus a search party, headed by Knevett, went back to the Westminster cellar. It was there, around midnight on Monday 4 November or perhaps in the small hours of 5 November, that a figure in a cloak and dark hat, booted and spurred as though for flight, was discovered skulking beneath the precincts of

Parliament. This 'very tall and desperate fellow' was immediately apprehended and bound fast. He gave his name as John Johnson, servant to Thomas Percy. It was a story that Guido Fawkes would maintain steadfastly for the next forty-eight hours.

The government's first warrant for arrest was issued in the name of Thomas Percy. He was described as a tall man with stooping shoulders, having 'a great broad beard' grizzled with white, and near-white hair: 'privy to one of the most horrible Treasons that ever was contrived'. It was stated to be essential 'to keep him alive' so that the rest of the conspirators could be discovered.[17] But Percy was mistakenly sought at Essex House rather than at his own lodging. It was then supposed that he had headed back to the north.

By this time the hubbub and commotion in the capital was swelling – not only in the Westminster area where the arrest had been made (and 'John Johnson' was being held in the King's chamber) but also in the Strand neighbourhood of the great lords' houses. These men were being turned out of their beds to fulfil their public responsibilities in a time of crisis. Thus Kit Wright overheard Lord Worcester, a Councillor, summoning Monteagle to go with him and 'call up' Northumberland. He rushed round to Tom Wintour at the Duck and Drake, crying 'the matter is discovered'. Wintour ordered him to make a further check and, when the hue and cry at Essex House was confirmed, correctly deduced that Percy was the man they were seeking. Wintour then told Kit Wright to hasten to Percy's lodging and 'bid him begone'. According to his confession, Tom Wintour added: 'I will stay and see the uttermost.'[18]

As news of the calamity which had befallen Guido spread among the conspirators still in London, a desperate dispersal commenced. Men fled on sweating horses, urged on by their panic-ridden masters. Fresh mounts would be needed along the way for in fleet horsemanship lay their only hope of eluding their pursuers. Kit Wright and Thomas Percy now went

together, Percy dramatically saying to a passing servant as he
went: 'I am undone.' At daylight Robert Keyes took to his
horse. At this point Rookwood and Tom Wintour were the
only conspirators left in London.* Rookwood was the next to
depart. He set out on an epic ride, thanks to his famous horsemanship and the unparalleled quality of his steeds he had
arranged along the way (he managed to ride thirty miles in two
hours on one horse: an amazing feat for both man and
animal). As a result he overtook Keyes, who had only got as
far as Highgate, and then Kit Wright and Percy at Little
Brickhill, north of Dunstable in Bedfordshire. Finally he caught
up with Catesby, Jack Wright and Bates further along the same
road. It was thus Rookwood who broke the news of the
disaster to Catesby, the man who had planned it all.

In the meantime Catesby and Jack Wright had had an
encounter of their own, with a recusant who was returning
from London called Henry Huddlestone. The young man's
father lived at Sawston Hall near Cambridge, but Henry, who
was related to the Vaux family, had installed his heavily pregnant wife at one of their houses near Harrowden. The meeting
was a most unfortunate chance from Huddlestone's point of
view, since although he was friendly with many of the conspirators – and had recently seen them in London – it is clear that
he knew nothing of what was being plotted. But he now rode
cheerfully along with Catesby and Wright. When Catesby's
horse lost a shoe at Dunstable and had to be reshod,
Huddlestone stayed with him. It was not until they met up
with Percy that Catesby bade Huddlestone 'go home to his
wife'.[19] From the point of view of the authorities, however,
Huddlestone had already been fatally contaminated by this
short, innocent journey.

With Rookwood reintegrated into the group – which
included Catesby and Bates, the Wright brothers and Percy –
six of the Plotters now rode on together in the direction of

---

* No one seems to have thought of contacting Francis Tresham, who since his
vain pleas that the action be abandoned was evidently no longer regarded as part
of the conspiracy.

Dunchurch. They were aided by horses sent out to them by Digby by prearrangement, Percy and Jack Wright throwing off their cloaks into the ditch to make for greater speed. At this point, however, Keyes hived off in the direction of Lord Mordaunt's house at Drayton where he used to live with his wife the governess, and went to ground in the neighbourhood.

Still the intrepid Tom Wintour lingered. With remarkable cool, he decided to go down to Westminster and find out for himself what was going on. He was, however, checked in King Street by a guard in the middle of the road who would not let him pass. He then overheard someone saying: 'There is a treason discovered in which the King and Lords were to have been blown up.' At this point Wintour really did know that all was lost.[20] He went to the stable which housed his gelding, and headed after his comrades. Unlike the superbly mounted Rookwood, however, he knew he had no chance of catching up with them before the rendezvous arranged by Catesby at Dunchurch. He therefore made for his brother Robert's house at Huddington, taking in Norbrook, home of his sister Dorothy Grant, on the way.

Catesby and his companions reached the family home at Ashby St Ledgers, on the road to Dunchurch, at about six o'clock in the evening. His mother Lady Catesby was at dinner, and Robert Wintour, who had ridden over from Huddington on his way to Dunchurch, was there too. According to Robert Wintour's testimony, Catesby sent a message that he should join him in the fields, at the edge of the town, bringing his horse: 'but that I should not let his mother know of his being there'. Robert Wintour duly kept the rendezvous. Catesby told him that 'Mr Fawkes was taken and the whole plot discovered.'[21]

This was the reality of it all. It says something for Catesby's courage, the fabulous misguided courage which had buoyed him up since the beginning of the whole mad enterprise and had acted like an elixir on his companions, that even now he had no idea of giving up. It was on to Dunchurch, where Catesby proceeded to persuade Digby, in the words of Milton's Lucifer: 'what though the field be lost, all is not lost'. Catesby admitted to the full dreadful details of the conspiracy, which, it is suggested, Digby did not know before. He admitted that the plan had been discovered and that they were all on the run. But, he stoutly maintained, they were still ahead of the game.

Even in his darkest hour, he fantasised of victory, Catesby announcing that the King and Salisbury were both dead. This must be their opportunity: 'if true Catholics would now stir, he doubted not that they might procure to themselves good conditions'. To Warwick for arms! To Norbrook where their own armaments were also stored! To Hewell Grange, home of Lord Windsor! To Grafton Manor, home of Robert Wintour's wealthy father-in-law John Talbot who would surely join them! Finally to the west and to Wales, where the restive Catholics would happily join with them...

Digby, whatever his private shock, was won over. He may not believed in what Catesby said, but he still believed in Catesby, his hero. Digby succumbed once again to Catesby's double evocation of their 'bonds of friendship' and the needs of the 'Cause'. But the party which now clattered on through the November darkness to carry out Catesby's grand plan at Warwick and so to the west was not much more than fifty people. It included the Wintours' step-brother, John, and Stephen Littleton, as well as Grant's friend, sworn to secrecy, Henry Morgan. The rest of Digby's hunting-party were appalled by the news that Catesby brought, and deeply resistant to any involvement with him. They correctly estimated his venture to be both treasonable to the state and ruinous to themselves. Then there were the 'lesser sort'. One of Digby's innocent servants, helpless in the face of his master's declared treachery, spoke for many when he asked what was going to happen to all of them, those who had never known the secret of 'this bloody faction' but now looked like being ruined by it.

Sir Everard Digby answered simply. No, he believed his servant had not known what was going on, 'but now there is no remedy'. George Prince, servant at the Red Lion Inn, remembered overhearing words of similar pessimism spoken by one of the conspirators at an open window. 'I doubt not but that we are all betrayed.'[22]

The London which the conspirators had left behind was in a state of confusion and apprehension. In the words of a contemporary observer: 'the common people muttered and imagined many things', and, as for the nobles, they knew not what to say or who to exonerate (or who to suspect): for a time 'a general jealousy possessed them all'. Running through all of this was a strain of wild if mindless rejoicing, for although it was certainly not clear who had been trying to do what and for why – except that the King had been saved from death – the crowd was not disposed to forego its traditional and exhilarating pastime of lighting bonfires in celebration. The Council made a virtue of necessity: there could be bonfires so long as they were 'without any danger or disorder'.[23] So the very first flames in commemoration of 'gunpowder, treason and plot', flames that would flicker on down the centuries, were lighted on 5 November 1605.

Obvious precautions were taken. The Lord Mayors of the City of London and of Westminster were ordered to set a civil watch upon their gates. The ports were all closed and did not reopen until 16 November. An embarrassing situation arose when the enthusiastic mob was found to be demonstrating outside the house of the Spanish Ambassador, assuming that the hated Spaniards were at the bottom of it all. The Council issued a hasty order that the Spanish Ambassador must not be 'touched with this horrible practice of treason', which was fair enough, given that he had planned to be present at the Opening of Parliament and would have perished with the others. In general the foreign ambassadors thought it politic to light their own bonfires of thanksgiving and throw money down into the crowd.[24] This went not only for the beleaguered Spaniard, and the Ambassador of the Catholic Archdukes, but also for the emissary of the Protestant Dutch: it was no time to be taking chances.

The Council, with Northumberland present, met in the

morning in an atmosphere of deepening perplexity concerning the Earl's position. He left the meeting believing that no restrictions had been placed upon his movements, while many of the lords believed equally strongly that he had been advised to rest quietly in his own house for the time being.*[25]

Northumberland's man Thomas Percy was the only name known for sure to be associated with the treason, other than that of the prisoner 'John Johnson'. Nothing illustrates the bizarre nature of this particular day better than two contrasting measures. On the one hand, someone sent off to Simon Foreman, the celebrated astrologer, to get him to work out the probable whereabouts of the fugitive, Percy. On the other hand, a search was put in hand for a collaborative Catholic priest who would persuade the prisoner Johnson that it was his duty to spill the beans.[26]

Parliament met briefly in the afternoon. The entry in the Commons' Journal for 5 November (crammed into a small space in the margin) was as follows:[27]

This last Night the Upper House of Parliament was searched by Sir Thomas Knevett; and one Johnson, Servant to Mr Thomas Percy was there apprehended; who had placed 36 Barrels of Gunpowder in the Vault under the House with a Purpose to blow the King, and the whole company, when they should there assemble.

Afterwards divers other Gentlemen were discovered to be of the Plot.†

Parliament was then prorogued until Saturday 9 March.

As the conspirators scattered and the Londoners wassailed, 'John Johnson' was being interrogated.[28] He had so far given away nothing beyond the bare facts that he was a Catholic

* Possibly Northumberland's deafness was responsible for this unfortunate mix-up at such a manifestly delicate moment in his fortunes.
† The original entry has been framed and today hangs in the 'Noes' voting lobby of the House of Commons, commemorating what might well have been the most dramatic day in Parliament's history. There is always a large circle of curious tourists and schoolchildren round it at times of public access.

from Netherdale in Yorkshire and that his father was called Thomas and his mother Edith Jackson (this at least was true) and that he was thirty-six years old (he was actually thirty-five). Certain scars noted on his body – presumably wounds received during his time as a soldier – he claimed to be the effects of pleurisy. A letter addressed to Guy Fawkes, and found in his possession, he explained neatly away by saying that Fawkes was one of his aliases.

Guido's composure was astonishing. Yes, he had intended to blow up the King and the Lords. No, he had no regrets – except the fact that he had not succeeded. 'The devil and not God', he said firmly, was responsible for the discovery of the Plot. No, he had not sought to warn the Catholic peers, he would have contented himself with praying for them. When the King asked 'Johnson' how he could 'conspire so hideous a treason' against the royal children, and so many souls which had never offended him, Guido did not attempt to deny the charge. He simply answered that a dangerous disease required a desperate remedy (an echo of Catesby's original words to Wintour, which suggest that the comforting catchphrase had been in general use among the conspirators).

Guido even had the ultimate bravado to tell some of the Scots present that his intention had been to blow them back into Scotland: his xenophobia remained unswerving. From time to time during the interrogation he smiled sorrowfully at his examiners, and told them they had not authority to examine him.

This iron self-control even evoked the admiration of King James. He described the prisoner as seeming to put on 'a Roman resolution': he was so constant and unshakeable in his grounds for action that the Councillors thought they had stumbled upon 'some new Mucius Scaevola born in England', comparing him to a legendary hero of Ancient Rome, who intended to assassinate the city's Etruscan enemy Lars Porsena, but slew the wrong man by mistake. Captured and hauled in front of Lars Porsena, Scaevola deliberately held his hand over the fire and let it be burnt off without flinching, in order to demonstrate that he would not give way under torture. In the legend, Lars Porsena was so impressed by Scaevola's endurance that he ordered his release and made peace with Rome.

The fate of Guy Fawkes, whatever the King's respect for his fortitude, was to be somewhat different.

CHAPTER TWELVE

The Gentler Tortures

The gentler tortures are to be first used unto him
[Guy Fawkes] ...
... and so God speed your good work. – James R

LETTER OF KING JAMES I
6 November 1605

The decision to apply torture to 'John Johnson' was taken by the King on 6 November.

Throughout the day the veteran Lord Chief Justice Sir John Popham pursued his investigations. Now in his mid-seventies, Popham was 'a huge, heavy, ugly man'. He was also implacable and 'inordinately cruel' in his hatred of the Catholics. His main line of attack was to go for those known Catholic subversives who had precipitately vanished from their usual haunts. Thus the servants of the extravagant, showy Ambrose Rookwood were examined on this day and his goods at Clopton – those incriminating crucifixes, beads and vestments – were seized.[1]

It is of course impossible to be certain how much of this process was helped on by Tresham's confidences to Monteagle, which were relayed forward. By the evening, however, the Lord Chief Justice had discovered enough to tell Salisbury that in addition to Percy he had 'pregnant suspicion ... concerning Robert Catesby, Ambrose Rookwood, one Keyes, Thomas Wynter [sic], John Wright and Christopher Wright and some suspicion of one Grant'.[2] Apart from Tresham, it will be seen that three names were missing at this stage: Digby, Robert

Wintour and Bates. The omission of Bates may be due to his inferior status, which made him less immediately interesting to the government. But the omission of Digby and Robert Wintour, both of whom operated in the midlands, suggests that the original source may well have been Francis Tresham, who from his London base would not necessarily have known of their involvement.

For all these advances, the obduracy of 'John Johnson' continued to enrage and baffle the authorities. Who on earth was he, with his scarred body and his mysterious past? Catholic subversives were supposed to be known to the government and closely watched, in an England which in its supervisory aspects met the criteria of a modern police state. But Guido stoutly maintained his false identity, allowing his comrades, as he hoped – if only it had been true! – time to get clear of the country.

Guido was now transferred to the Tower of London. The King himself drew up a list of questions that were to be put to him there, headed by the vital question '*as to what he is*, For I can never yet hear of any man that knows him'. After that, there followed many others including 'When and where he learned to speak French?' and 'If he was a Papist, who brought him up in it?' (There was evidently a strong suspicion that this 'John Johnson' was a Catholic priest.)[3]

The decision to put Guido to the torture was one that needed the authority either of the King or of the Privy Council, using the royal prerogative. King James himself took an active interest in the whole topic and his rights of decision in the matter. When Ralegh had been arrested in 1603 for possible conspiracy in the Main Plot, it had been the King who 'gave charge no torture should be used'. In the case of 'John Johnson', he reached a different decision.

Torture as such was contrary to English common law, or, as Sir Edward Coke in his capacity as a jurist would write in his *Third Institute*: 'there is no law to warrant tortures in this land'.*

* In 1215 Magna Carta, that cornerstone of English liberties, had expressly forbidden torture (Jardine, *Torture*, p. 48).

Coke, who was now in his fifties, had been the Attorney-General since 1594. (Before that, he had been in turn Solicitor-General and Speaker of the House of Commons.) He was a man who thoroughly understood the ways of the world, having married two extremely rich women. The second of these, Lady Hatton, twenty-six years his junior, was rich in connections too, being a member of the Cecil family. Immensely skilful – if at the same time pitiless and unscrupulous – he would in the words of Aubrey 'play with a case as a cat would with a mouse'.[4]

What Coke blandly ignored, in his emphasis on the rule of law, was that use of torture, supported by the royal prerogative, had actually been on the increase in England under the Tudors. Far from being a mediaeval survival, torture was one of the novel weapons in the armoury of Henry VIII's servant Thomas Cromwell, who had seemingly learnt much about this useful European practice during his travels abroad for Cardinal Wolsey.[5]

Torture was in theory reserved for exceptional circumstances, but, since these special circumstances included any suggestion of treason, a long list of Catholic priests had suffered frightfully in the time of Queen Elizabeth. (They were subject to torture, the government was careful to point out, not for their religion but for their supposed treason.) Among the leading characters in this narrative, both Father John Gerard and Little John had been tortured in the 1590s.

The uncovering of any conspiracy – and there had been a great number of them under Elizabeth, connected to the rescue of Mary Queen of Scots – was bound to be followed by the avid use of torture. Francis Throckmorton, a cousin of Catesby and Tresham, had been 'often racked' for his part in a plot of 1583. Then there were the servants of great men, such as those of the Duke of Norfolk, whom Burghley discreetly had tortured, under 'the Queen's signet'. Thomas Norton, the rackmaster, was said to have boasted of pulling one unfortunate fellow, called Alexander Briant, 'one good foot longer than ever God made him'. Sometimes there was not even the excuse of treason. Gypsies were tortured in Bridewell in 1596 to answer the truth about their 'lewd behaviour'; a boy Humfrey was 'lightly tortured' (no arms to be dislocated) in Nottingham for suspected complicity in a burglary.[6]

Such indiscriminate use – and the fact that it was against common law – made for a lingering popular uneasiness on the subject of torture. In 1592 the 'often exercise of the rack in the Tower' was said to be 'odious and much spoken of by the people'.* This uneasiness was not of course shared by the authorities, who were in the business of extracting information as fast as possible. Another method of applying pressure was by starvation, known as 'pinching'. Prisoners – including priests – would be incarcerated without food or water in dark subterranean dungeons, the only moisture being drops falling from the dank roof.[7]

This method took time to produce results. For those who were investigating a genuinely treasonable conspiracy, speed might be of the essence in probing its depths, as was undoubtedly the case with the dangerous criminal 'John Johnson'. Yet it is notable that Thomas Norton finally got into trouble for going beyond the permissible limits regarding torture and was forced to explain that he had not actually carried out his grotesque boast about lengthening Alexander Briant, but had only *threatened* to carry it out. In any case he had admired the 'poor unlearned' fellow's courage. (Briant was in fact not so poor and unlearned: he was a disguised priest.)[8]

Torture of course had its rules. No one was supposed to be tortured to death: this would have been counter-productive apart from anything else. For this reason, maimed or mutilated people – such as Little John since his accident – were not supposed to be subjected to it because they might be too weak to survive. If a session failed to provide the desired information,

* It should be pointed out that England was not alone in the practice. The Spanish Inquisition – the 'Holy Office' – employed torture: this was one of the aspects of England's hereditary Catholic enemy, Spain, which had aroused disgust and horror among the English, especially those merchants who might fall foul of the Inquisition, during the reign of Elizabeth I.

the victim should not in theory be tortured over and over again, on the reasonable assumption that he might not have had the information in the first place, and therefore had no truthful means of ending his torment. This was a rule which was generally ignored, especially in the case of priests. Lastly, torture was supposed to be increased gradually.

The letter which the King signed on 6 November specified that for 'such a desperate fellow' as John Johnson, if he would not otherwise confess, 'the gentler Tortures are to be first used unto him *et sic per gradus ad ima tenditur*' – and so by degrees proceeding to the worst. He concluded, 'and so God speed your good work', signing himself 'James R' (see plate section).[9] The gentler tortures referred to the manacles and the worst to the rack. By the 1590s, the manacles had become the method most favoured by the authorities, as they were inexpensive and easy to operate for those who applied them. The traitor – or suspect – was hung up by his wrists against a wall, using iron gauntlets which could be gradually tightened; wood supports beneath the feet would be removed and the prisoner would be left dangling for several hours, sometimes longer. As the vicious Richard Topcliffe observed of Campion (whom he tortured more than ten times): 'it will be as though he were dancing a trick or figure'. There were survivors of the manacles – notably Father Gerard – but there were also those such as his fellow Jesuit Father Henry Walpole whose hands were permanently maimed.[10]

There was only one rack in England, housed at the Tower of London. The rack was a large open frame of oak, raised from the ground. The prisoner was laid on it with his back to the floor, his wrists and ankles attached by cords to rollers at either end. Levers were operated which stretched the prisoner, quite slowly, while he was urged to confess. The rack, inevitably, caused permanent damage and dislocation to the prisoner. So feared was the instrument, indeed, that sometimes the mere sight of it was enough to cow the prisoner into giving information.[11]

It is not absolutely certain that in the case of Guy Fawkes

the authorities proceeded from manacles to the rack, although the King's letter clearly envisaged that it might be necessary to move on to 'the worst', in order to break this iron man. Sir Edward Hoby, a well-informed observer and a Gentleman of the Privy Chamber, wrote to Brussels that only the manacles had been used. 'Yet the common voice', in the words of Father Gerard, 'was that he was extremely racked in the first few days.' Priests subsequently held in the Tower certainly heard that Fawkes had been racked, and observers who saw Guido on the next occasion he was displayed in public witnessed a sick man, utterly broken in body.[12] Thus the balance of probability is in favour of the rack. Men did manage to hold out against the manacles – and Guido was nothing if not strong – but against the rack never, or hardly ever.

What is certain is that some time on 7 November, following the application of torture, they broke him – they broke Guido's body and in so doing they broke at last his spirit.* Hoby had a meaningful phrase for it: 'Since Johnson's being in the Tower, he beginneth to speak English.' His courage was still high the night before, as Sir William Waad, Lieutenant of the Tower, reported to Salisbury.[13] (As Lieutenant, Waad was always present at these sessions of torture.)

Guido's conversation with Waad was revealing. Here was no common criminal but, in a certain warped way, an idealist – or perhaps fanatic was the appropriate word: 'He [Johnson] told us that since he undertook this action he did every day pray to God he might perform that which might be for the advancement of[1] the Catholic Faith and saving his own soul.' To explain his silence, Guido revealed that he had taken an oath to say nothing in company with his (so far nameless) comrades, and they had all then partaken of the Sacrament. But he

---

* There is a lack of documentary evidence to show conclusively where Guy Fawkes was held and tortured; traditionally he was held in the Bloody Tower, but tortured in the White Tower, in rooms below the present wooden (ground) floor; he may also have been held in a room, now vanished, in what looks like the thickness of the wall. Prisoners, in general, were tortured in subterranean areas and often held near by in advance to maximise the terror (Geoffrey Parnell, Keeper of Tower History, to the author; Yeoman Warders to the author).

was careful to add that the (similarly nameless) priest who gave them the Sacrament 'knew nothing about it'.[14] This oath had been sworn, and this illegal Sacrament administered, in England, which of course whetted the appetite of his interrogators. Nevertheless Guido still hoped to be able to endure long enough not to have to break his vow.

To Waad's amazement, Guido even managed to pass the night of 6 November resting peacefully 'as a man devoid of all trouble of mind' – although he had been warned of what lay in store for him. Waad told the prisoner that 'if he held his resolution of mind to be so silent', he must realise that the state was equally resolved to proceed with that severity which was necessary in a case of such great consequence. 'Therefore I willed him to prepare himself.'[15]

Having held out with a staunchness which did indeed recall the legendary determination of Scaevola, Guido cracked. He began to talk, probably late on 7 November, and continued on the 8th and 9th.

There was only one problem with all this. As the historian Tacitus had wisely observed fifteen hundred years before Guido was taken to that dark, underground chamber in the Tower, torture tended to bring about false witness.*[16] In order to alleviate his sufferings, the tormented man was more likely to give the Council the details it wanted to hear, rather than a strictly truthful account of what had taken place.

On 6 November, with Guido still holding out, Catesby and his confederates in the midlands must be judged to have had at least a chance of escape, although they would no doubt have left a wake of destruction behind them when the innocent – wives, families and uninvolved recusants – were picked up to pay for the crimes of the guilty. In any case it was not an option that Catesby considered. The mad scramble for further arms, further horses and further adherents continued, but it continued without success.

---

* Torture was a judicial procedure that had been known among the Romans, when slaves were frequently subjected to it.

The raid on Warwick Castle did secure some horses, but it also provoked the second public proclamation by the government, which was issued the next day. This named as wanted men, in addition to Percy: Catesby, Rookwood, Thomas Wintour, the two Wrights, John Grant (misnamed Edward Grant) and Robert Ashfield, servant to Catesby (probably a mistake for Bates). Rather touchingly under the circumstances, Robert Wintour had denounced the raid on Warwick because it would make 'a great uproar' in the county. Rookwood was against it for quite a different reason and skirted the town: with his magnificent equestrian cortège, he had no need of further horses.[17]

After a visit to Norbrook to pick up the stored arms, the conspirators headed in the direction of Huddington. At this point Catesby ordered Thomas Bates to make a detour and break the news to Father Garnet and his fellow priests at Coughton Court. In his letter to Garnet, Catesby once again showed that blind faith in the rightness of what he was doing – and had done – which was singularly out of touch with the reality of the recusant position. Catesby, together with Digby, asked Father Garnet to excuse their rashness, but then proceeded to solicit Garnet's assistance to raise a party in Wales where, far from the centre of government, Catholic support was believed to be vigorous. Garnet was appalled. With the arrival of Father Tesimond, Bates overheard the despairing words: 'we are all utterly undone'.[18]

The priests understood quite well what was going to happen, and so did poor Mary Digby. When Father Garnet tried to comfort her she burst out weeping, as well she might, with her glorious young husband a traitor and, almost worse, her two little boys as traitor's sons. Garnet's reply to Catesby and Digby begged them to desist from their 'wicked actions' and listen to the preachings of the Pope.[19]

Eliza Vaux, at Harrowden with Father Gerard and two other priests, Father Singleton and Father Strange, had got wind of the catastrophe the night before. It was brought to her by her young cousin (and tenant) Henry Huddlestone, who had had that ominous encounter with Catesby and others on the road as they fled. At the time it was thought safer to pretend she had heard it via the servants' network, from one of Sir Griffin Markham's men to one of hers. Eliza was still intent on the marriage of her son Edward to Lord Suffolk's daughter. She had been about to send him up to London to further the protracted negotiations when she heard that there were some 'garboils' (disturbances) in the capital and held him back.[20] With a sinking heart, Eliza realised that there was now little point in a Catholic Romeo trying to further his suit with Lord Suffolk's Juliet.

A more immediate problem was the plight of the priests. Harrowden, like any known recusant centre, might expect to be searched imminently. There was also the general Harrowden concern for Father Garnet, at Coughton. So Father Singleton and Father Strange, accompanied by Henry Huddlestone (who left his pregnant wife behind at Harrowden), set out on the morning of 7 November. On reaching Warwick, however, they found it heavily patrolled following the raid of the night before. Attempting to make a circuit, they were stopped and arrested at Kenilworth by Sir Richard Verney.

Since Sir Richard was uncle to Eliza's new son-in-law, Sir George Symeon, Eliza was full of hope that she could get the prisoners released. But the situation was too serious for cosy family connections to operate — and recusant connections could in any case be an embarrassment. Furthermore Eliza, in sending desperate messages to Sir Richard, naively issued full physical descriptions of her friends — since she had no idea under what aliases they were being held (while fervently denying that any of them could possibly be priests).[21] Coolly, Verney passed all this on to Salisbury. Huddlestone and Father Strange were taken to the Tower, and Father Singleton to Bridewell prison. Meanwhile the household at Harrowden — including Father Gerard — awaited the inevitable arrival of the poursuivants. At least Father Garnet managed to vanish from the authorities' sight for the next few weeks into the thin recusant air. Anne Vaux was able to join him, posing as his sister

Mrs Perkins.[22] The Superior of the Jesuits was safe – or so it seemed at the time.

The leading conspirators – those who were left – and their diminishing band of helpers continued on their route to Huddington, where, according to Gertrude Wintour's subsequent testimony, they arrived at about two o'clock in the afternoon on 6 November.* Here they were joined by Tom Wintour. Even among the Wintours' closest relations and neighbours, there was no sympathy for the cause, only horror at the past and fear for the future. Thomas Habington of Hindlip, who had his wife Mary and their new-born son William to protect as well as priests, refused to have anything to do with the fugitives, and forbade his household to show any sympathy. Father Edward Oldcorne, among those he was sheltering, was equally horrified. Only Father Tesimond, the lively 'cholerick' Yorkshireman, seems to have had some concern for his friends' plight, even if he did not share their objectives. He came back with Bates from Coughton to join Catesby at Huddington for a while. (Danger did not however diminish his sense of style: Henry Morgan would later testify that Tesimond had been wearing 'coloured satin done with gold lace' on this occasion.)[23]

On 7 November the Archpriest Father Blackwell issued a passionate public statement which was far more in keeping with the sentiments of these honest Catholics than the wild do-or-die statements the conspirators were still making. Blackwell denounced the Plot against the King, the Prince and the nobility as 'intolerable, uncharitable, scandalous and desperate'. He was horrified by the news that a Catholic – he meant Guido – had been privy to 'this detestable device'. Father Blackwell hastened to point out that according to Catholic doctrine it was

---

* There are various traditions at Huddington associated with this dramatic arrival: Gertrude Wintour is supposed to have stationed herself at her window, waiting for the messenger from London: if he waved his hat when he came into view, all was well, but if he rode with his head covered, all was lost. An inscription on a windowpane in the main bedchamber, 'past cark [hope], past care', may refer to Gertrude's despair. 'Lady Wintour's Walk' in the woods is said to be haunted by her restless ghost. (Huddington owner to the author; Hamilton, I, pp. 182–3.)

not lawful for 'private subjects, by private authority, to take arms against their lawful king', even if he turned into a tyrant. He hammered home the message still further by referring to the duty of priests to instruct their flocks that 'private, violent attempts' could never be justified; Catholics must not support them in any way.[24]

For the conspirators, even if they had time to be aware of the Archpriest's proclamation, all this was the useless language of passive endurance which they had long ago rejected. In the small hours of the Tuesday morning, 7 November – as early as three o'clock – all those left at Huddington Court including the servants went to confession before taking the Sacrament at Mass. It was an indication, surely, that none of them now expected to live very long. Then they rode out into the rainy darkness, thirty-six of them all told. At midday they were at Hewell Grange, the house of the fourteen-year-old Lord Windsor (Northampton's ward), who was not there. It was still raining heavily. They helped themselves to arms, gunpowder and a large store of money. But the local villagers gazed at them with sullen hostility. On being told that the conspirators stood for 'God and Country', the reply came back that round Hewell Grange, men were for 'King James as well as God and Country'. Digby admitted later that 'not one man' joined them at this stage.[25] Their expectations of gathering support had been moonshine.

At ten o'clock that night, the band arrived at Holbeach House, near Kingswinford, just inside Staffordshire. It was the home of Stephen Littleton, one of those from the hunting-party who had actually stuck with them, and it was a house they believed could be fortified. For some time the Plotters had been aware of being followed. For a moment a hope sprang up that these were reinforcements, but it was a wild hope. It was in fact the *posse comitatus* (vigilante force) of the High Sheriff of Worcestershire, Sir Richard Walsh, accompanied by 'the power and face of the county'.

Tom Wintour now elected to beard the venerable John Talbot of Grafton, Gertrude Wintour's father, and see if there might not be some help forthcoming from that source. (Robert Wintour had pointedly refused to do so while they were still at Huddington, saying that everyone knew that John Talbot could not be drawn away from his loyal allegiance to the King.) Stephen Littleton went with Tom. None of this did any good. John Talbot was at his Shropshire home of Pepperhill about ten miles from Holbeach. He repelled them angrily, saying that the visit 'might be as much as his life was worth', adding, 'I pray you get hence.'[26] It was while these two were away on their fruitless mission that a horrible accident took place at Holbeach House, which in the taut and eerie atmosphere seems to have changed the mood there from one of bravado to despair.

The gunpowder taken away from Whewell Grange, conveyed in an open cart, had suffered from the drenching rain. It was now spread out in front of the fire at Holbeach to dry, which was an extraordinarily rash thing to do. One gets the impression that the Plotters were by now all so tired, as well as desperate – they had been riding on and on and on, some of them, like Catesby himself, seeking not only arms but sanctuary for the last three nights – that they were hardly aware of what they were doing. At any rate a spark flew out of the fire and the gunpowder ignited. So Catesby got his powder explosion at last. It was a quick violent blaze which engulfed him, together with Rookwood, John Grant and the latter's friend (from the Dunchurch hunting-party), Henry Morgan. The night before Robert Wintour had had a dream of premonition: 'He thought he saw steeples stand awry, and within those churches strange and unknown faces.' When he saw the scorched faces of his comrades, he recognised them as the faces in his dream.[27]

As Wintour and Stephen Littleton were on their way back to Holbeach, a man brought them a message, which suggested that these conspirators were dead, and the rest of the company 'dispersed'. At this point Littleton's determination gave out – he had after all been a latecomer to the enterprise. He encouraged Tom Wintour to fly 'and so would he'. Wintour, however, showed his usual stubborn resolve. He refused to turn away. 'I told him I would first see the body of my friend [Catesby] and bury him, whatsoever befell me.' Wintour went on alone.[28]

When he arrived at Holbeach, however, he found that the messenger had exaggerated the disaster. It was true that Digby had vanished – in fact he went with the intention of giving himself up – and so had Robert Wintour, who would eventually join up with Stephen Littleton. John Wintour, the step-brother, who felt he had blundered into the conspiracy by mistake, slipped away during the night hours and gave himself up. The servant Thomas Bates had gone: no pressure was now being put on the Plotters to remain together. But Catesby at least was 'reasonably well' and so was Rookwood, although John Grant had been so badly disfigured by the fire – 'his eyes burnt out' – that he was blind. Morgan had also been burnt. The remainder of the company consisted of the two Wright brothers, Jack and Kit, stalwart to the last, as they had been among the first of the Plotters, and Thomas Percy. Wintour asked them what they intended to do.

'We mean here to die,' was the unyielding reply.

Wintour answered with equal firmness: 'I will take such part as you do.'

It would not be long now. Sir Richard Walsh and his two hundred men were closing in on Holbeach. On the morning of Friday 8 November, as Guido in the Tower prepared painfully to make the first of his major confessions, his erstwhile comrades readied themselves for the end. The devastating chance of the explosion had convinced them that their deaths were fast approaching, and so they all started to pray: 'the Litanies and such like'. Then Catesby, taking the gold crucifix which always hung round his neck, and kissing it, said that he had undertaken everything only for 'the honour of the Cross' and the True Faith which venerated that Cross. He now expected to give his life for that same cause, since he saw it was not God's will that they should succeed as they had planned. Yet he would not be taken prisoner: 'against that only he would defend himself with his sword'.[29]

The company under Walsh arrived in front of Holbeach

about eleven o'clock to besiege the house. Walsh was afterwards criticised for keeping himself 'close under the wall' for safety's sake, although such a quantity of men, armed with muskets, could hardly be said to be in any great danger, nor could the issue of the siege be in much doubt. Almost immediately Tom Wintour, crossing the courtyard, was shot in the shoulder, which cost him the use of his arm. The second shot dropped Jack Wright; Kit Wright was hit next. Their famous swordsmanship had availed them little against the muskets' fire. After that, Ambrose Rookwood, still suffering from the effects of the fire, was also hit.

There were now left, as possible defenders, Catesby and Percy, as well as the wounded Tom Wintour, the blinded John Grant and the burnt Henry Morgan.

'Stand by me, Mr Tom,' said Robin Catesby, 'and we will die together.'

'I have lost the use of my right arm,' answered Wintour, 'and I fear that will cause me to be taken.' Even so, the two stood close together for their last stand, along with Percy, at the door of the house by which their assailants would enter. Robin Catesby and Thomas Percy were then brought down together by the same lucky shot. (John Streete of Worcester, who fired the shot, later petitioned for a thousand-pounds reward for this feat, although it was certainly by chance rather than design.)[30] Then the besiegers rushed in. What happened next was a macabre kind of rout, in which common sense – these men were wanted criminals – and even humanity, took second place to brutish greed.*

The Wright brothers and Percy were clearly *in extremis* but might just possibly have been kept alive, despite their 'many and grievous wounds', if there had been a surgeon available. Instead, their moribund bodies were crudely stripped: the Ensign of the posse himself pulled off Kit Wright's boots and

---

* According to local tradition, Stephan Littleton's young groom, Gideon Grove, managed to mount a horse and break out of the courtyard in the confusion of fire and smoke; he got as far as some fenland near Wombourne where the soldiers caught and killed him. His ghost, as commemorated in a ballad by the nineteenth-century Rhymer Greensill, is said to haunt the spot as a 'Phantom Rider'. (*Black Country Bugle*, October–November 1972; local information to the author.)

fine silk stockings. It was a distasteful scene. Sir Thomas Lawley, who was assisting Walsh, commented on it afterwards to Salisbury, when he referred to the unpleasant lack of discipline of 'the baser sort'. Percy died fairly quickly, thus fulfilling the explanation of Simon Foreman, the astrologer consulted after his flight: 'Saturn, being Lord of the 8th house [of death] sheweth that the fugitive shall be taken by the commandment of the Prince, and in being taken, shall be slain.'[31] If the Wrights lingered longer, it was not to any purpose; lying there naked on their way to death, they had neither the voice nor the energy to explain why and what they had done.

Grant and Morgan, both damaged by the fire, were easily captured, as was Ambrose Rookwood, who was not only scorched but wounded by musket fire. Tom Wintour, the first to fall, seems to have been saved by the action of the Sheriff's assistant, Lawley, and Lawley's servant. Afterwards there was a squabble about Wintour's horse, which the rival Sheriff of Staffordshire tried in vain to claim. But at the time Lawley at least had some practical sense of duty, realising that the conspirators, taken alive, would do 'better service' to the King than their speechless bodies.[32] Wintour was at first manhandled and beaten and probably stabbed in his stomach by a pike. Then someone came from behind, caught his arms, including the wounded one, and made him prisoner.

Robin Catesby survived long enough to crawl painfully inside the house. There he managed to find a picture of the Virgin Mary, and it was clutching this in his arms that he finally died. Lawley, who had denigrated the plunderers, saw himself in a different light when he collected up Catesby's gold crucifix and the picture of the Virgin, together with any other religious items he could find. Naturally, these were not despatched to the bereaved Lady Catesby at Ashby St Ledgers, the mother to whom Robin, on his fiery course, had not wished to say goodbye. To Lawley, these were not devotional emblems but valuable trophies. He sent them up to London to demonstrate just the kind of 'superstitious and Popish idols' which had inspired the rebels.[33]

So Tom Wintour's worst fears had come about. He had not died with his beloved Robin Catesby and he had lived on, in whatever lacerated state, to tell the tale of the Powder Treason. But Catesby, whose gallantry and rashness had dazzled and seduced a generation of young Catholic men, had had his last wish fulfilled. He had died without being 'taken'. Not for Catesby the Tower of London and its rigours, nor for him the pitiless indignities of a traitor's death. Of the two of them, Robin and Tom, it was Catesby who was the lucky one.

In London, the confused frenzy which had gripped almost everyone from King to commoner in the first two days after the discovery of the Plot was beginning to subside. Even before the news of the Holbeach shoot-out reached the capital, the general feeling of actually being endangered – where would they strike next? – was fading. Yet the government made it clear that no chances were being taken. On 7 November, while Percy was still at liberty, his patron the Earl of Northumberland was placed under house arrest, in the care of the Archbishop of Canterbury at Lambeth Palace.

On the same day, the gunpowder 'from out the vault of the Parliament House' was transported to the Tower of London. Here it was deposited in 'His Majesty's Store within the office of Ordnance', not very far from where Guido was incarcerated in his subterranean chamber. The gunpowder was described in the official receipt in the Debenture Book of the Royal Ordnance as having been 'laid and placed for the blowing up of the said house [Parliament] and the destruction of the King's Majesty, the nobility, and commonality there assembled'. Together with a couple of iron crowbars, eighteen hundredweight of powder was received.[34]

Interestingly enough, the powder was described officially as 'decayed'. A cynical clerk in the Royal Ordnance might have reflected that the danger to the King and all the rest of them had not really been so great after all. This powder (unlike the wretched stuff which had burnt up the conspirators at Holbeach) would not have exploded anyway. The straightforward explanation for this failure in the Plotters' arrangements is that the powder had once again separated in its elements – as had happened previously – and that Guido had simply not realised the fact (unless of course the 'decay' had taken place in the two days following 5 November). A rider to this, of a more Machiavellian nature, involves the Earl of Salisbury. One may question whether he really tolerated with equanimity the presence of a substance such as gunpowder in the vault at Westminster, in such large quantities and for so long. Perhaps a discreet search had established that the powder no longer constituted a real threat to anyone – except of course to Guy Fawkes himself by incriminating him.

Now that the government was so demonstrably on the winning side, an amazing quantity of people of all sorts, high and low, stepped forward to flag their loyalty by providing information. One of the first to do so was Lady Tasborough, mother-in-law to Agnes Lady Wenman, the bosom friend of Eliza Vaux. She thought it helpful to communicate the contents of that fatal letter of April which, it will be remembered, she had opened in her daughter-in-law's absence. On 5 November itself Lord Chief Justice Popham was already able to communicate to Salisbury details of Eliza's unfortunate prophecy – 'we shall see Tottenham turn French' – which proved that she 'expected something was about to take place'. Popham's comments on this were not encouraging for Eliza's future. Since two Jesuits, Gerard and Whalley (an alias for Garnet), made Harrowden 'the chiefest place of their access', therefore 'she may know somewhat'.[35] All this was in advance of Henry Huddlestone's capture and Eliza's frantic efforts to free the priests, which scarcely improved her chances of eluding the attentions of the Privy Council.

Others rapidly discounted any connection to the traitors. There were, for example, those who stepped forward gratuitously to point out – in case there was any doubt – that they had not seen the conspirators for at least ten years. Where Catholicism was concerned, Ben Jonson reflected cynically that immediately after the Plot's discovery there were 'five hundred gentlemen less' professing that religion. On 7 November, Jonson himself, uneasily aware of his known connection to the Plotters, came before the Privy Council. He had tried to contact an undercover priest who wanted a safe conduct in exchange for information but had failed to find him, in spite of the help of the (Catholic) chaplain to the Venetian Ambassador.

Two days later Sir Walter Ralegh (whose wife, Elizabeth Throckmorton, was a first cousin of Lady Catesby) utterly denied any connection with the recent treason, which he said he would have given his life to uncover. He recalled to mind his many services to his country, and desperately tried to distance himself from a plot which he termed 'this more than devilish invention'. On the same day, the Earl of Dorset, father-in-law of Viscount Montague, asked him anxiously whether he had known anything 'either directly or indirectly' which would have stopped him coming to Parliament.[36]

All the while Guy Fawkes sweated in the Tower, first to resist his torturers, then to give them in some measure what they wanted – or at any rate enough to relieve his torment. So far as the evidence can be pieced together, he revealed his true identity on 7 November and said that the Plot was confined to five (unnamed) people. His important confession was that on 8 November.[37] This confession named at last names, although it did not identify any Catholic priests. Nor for that matter did Guido incriminate prominent English Catholics or reveal the identity of the Protector, although he did talk at length about the plans for the proclamation of the Princess Elizabeth.

The third confession of 9 November, attested in front of Commissioners on 10 November, must be assumed to be the product of prolonged bouts of torture, growing increasingly severe.[38] Guido named Francis Tresham at this point, although he ascribed to him a comparatively minor role, and he named the priest who had administered the Sacrament following the oath as Father Gerard (but Guido stuck to his point that Gerard had not known what was going on). It is quite possible that Salisbury was present at this session since Waad wrote to him, saying that Fawkes wanted to see him. At all events, one new revelation was exactly what Salisbury wanted to hear. Here at last as a result of torture was the name – or so Coke would pretend later – of the government's *bête noire*, Hugh Owen of Flanders.

The signatures of Fawkes, declining in strength and coherence as the interrogation proceeded, provide, even today, their own mute testimonial to what he suffered (see plate section). The last 'Guido' – his chosen name, his name of exile – was scarcely more than a scrawl, and little helpless jabs of the pen beside it showed what it had cost Fawkes even to write as much as this.

CHAPTER THIRTEEN

Fire and Brimstone

~

It may well be called a roaring, nay a thundering sin
of fire and brimstone, from the which God hath so
miraculously delivered us all.

KING JAMES
to Parliament, 9 November 1605

King James' speech to Parliament on Saturday 9
November was a fine flowery piece of oratory. As the
discoverer of the Plot, he certainly blew his own
trumpet royally.[1] At the same time, he showed courage – he
did after all believe that he had been the intended victim of an
explosion only four days earlier. Even more admirably, James
showed himself merciful towards the English Catholics who
had not been involved in the Powder Treason as it did not
follow 'that all professing the Romish religion were guilty of
the same'. The 'seduced' Papists could still be good subjects.
He expressly mentioned the fact that the souls of some
Catholics would be saved and criticised the harshness of the
Puritans 'that will admit no salvation to any Papist'.

Although this policy of mildness and conciliation faded, as
the extent of the Jesuit priests' involvement – their alleged
involvement – was signalled by a vengeful government, it is as
well to remember that the Powder Treason was in the early
days seen by the King for exactly what it was: the work of a
few Catholic fanatics.

Naturally King James recalled his own troubled history.
Monarchs, 'like the high Trees', were subject to more tempests

40

than ordinary mortals, and the King himself had suffered from more tempests than most monarchs: he had been first threatened 'while I was yet in my mother's belly'. Now God had miraculously delivered them all from 'a roaring, nay a thundering sin of fire and brimstone'.

Then the King outlined the various unique elements which went to make up this particular treason. First, there was the sheer cruelty of the Plot itself which had threatened to destroy so many innocent people with no distinction made 'of young nor of old, of great nor of small, of man nor of woman'. Considering the various ways of putting mankind to death, he had no hesitation in picking on fire as the 'most raging and merciless', because there was no pity to be expected and no appeal against it. (A man might pity his fellow man at the last moment, and in any case a defence could be mounted; as to the 'unreasonable' wild animals, even the lions pitied Daniel ...)*

The second element was one on which some might have had other views. The King insisted that there were small grounds if any to justify the conspiracy – only religion, and that was scarcely enough. The third element was the truly miraculous one, and on this the King really let himself go. This was his own unequalled brilliance in discerning what was about to happen. Regardless of his own trusting nature – 'I ever did hold Suspicion to be the sickness of a Tyrant' – he had been inspired to interpret the Monteagle Letter as indicating 'this horrible form of blowing us up all by Powder'.

The King solemnly told the assembled peers that he would have had one consolation if the Plot had succeeded. At least he would have died 'in the most Honourable and best company', rather than in 'an ale-house or a stew' (a brothel). Concerning the conspirators, he quoted another King, the Biblical David:

* This, the King's preeminent point, makes it clear that it was the fact of the terrorist plan being both random in its effect and inexorable in its execution which was found specially shocking, in exactly the same way as it is found shocking today about terrorist activities, which are usually pointed out to be cowardly as well as wicked.

'they had fallen into the trap which they themselves had made'. Moving on from the Bible to Ancient Rome he emphasised the need for thanksgiving. For if Scipio, 'an Ethnic [that is, neither Jewish nor Christian] led only by the light of Nature', had called on his people to give thanks for his victory over Hannibal, how much more necessary was it for Christians to express their gratitude! 'The Mercy of God is above all his works,' said the King.

In the House of Commons, the point was well taken. Sir Edward Hexter moved that the Speaker of the House 'should make manifest the thankfulness of the House to God, for his [the King's] safe Deliverance'. For the future, 'they would all, and every one of them be ready with the uttermost Drop of their Blood'. Parliament was now once more prorogued – until 21 January 1606 – since, as the King pointed out, all their energies would be needed in the unravelling of the recent wicked conspiracy. The chosen day was, incidentally, a Tuesday, like 5 August 1600 and 5 November 1605. Since the King had twice been 'delivered' on this propitious day of the week, he thought it 'not amiss' that the experiment of meeting on a Tuesday should be repeated.[2]

Salisbury was left to write to the English ambassadors abroad an elaborate letter of explanation of what had occurred. These included Edmondes in Brussels, Parry in Paris and Cornwallis in Spain. Fortunately King James had taken pains in his speech to establish that the Catholic foreign powers were not suspected of complicity – 'no King or Prince of honour will ever abase himself so much'. The government proclamation against the conspirators had indeed ended with the most slavish defence of the Catholic powers' integrity: 'we cannot admit so inhumane a thought as their involvement'. The way was open for these rulers to send back to London formal expressions of sheer horror at what had been so grossly plotted.[3]

Of course the powers and potentates revealed their own preoccupations. The Duke of Lerma, the Spanish King's *privado* (favourite), while describing the conspirators as 'atheists and

43

devils', hoped to hear that there were also Puritans 'in the mixture'. Zuñiga, the Spanish envoy in London (he who had prudently lit bonfires and thrown money to the crowd on 5 November), believed that Thomas Percy had been in charge of the operation and that he was 'a heretic', in other words a Protestant, who was known to favour France over Spain. With equal conviction and equal inaccuracy the French King was quite sure that the Spanish ministers must have had a hand 'in so deep a practice'.[4]

On Sunday 10 November, Salisbury, armed with Guido's confession, was able at last to set in motion proceedings to extradite Hugh Owen from Flanders. Owen angrily rebutted the charge: 'I would take my oath', he wrote to Lerma in Spain, that he had known nothing about the conspiracy. The cautious Archdukes, worried by the lack of proof, contented themselves with putting Owen and his secretary under house arrest.[5]

Much more gratifying for the government was the sermon of the Bishop of Rochester, Dr Barlow, at Paul's Cross on this same Sunday. It was to be the first in a long line of such exhortatory sermons on the subject of the Powder Treason. Described as 'one of the ripest in learning', Barlow had been part of the team associated with producing the Authorised Version of the Bible after the Hampton Court conference. Since he, like the King, would have been present in the House of Lords at the moment of the explosion, his awareness of his own narrow escape must have lent him a particular fervour. In any case Barlow, a man who had already given two sermons at Paul's Cross, one praising Essex on his return from Ireland in 1596, and another justifying his execution five years later (with detailed instructions from Salisbury), had surely been primed over what to say.[6]

Yet again the party line was to vilify Guy Fawkes, and to see the Plot as the work of fanatics. In contrast to many, many subsequent sermons, the English Catholics were not attacked as such, just as King James had been careful to distinguish good Papists from bad. But the main thrust of Barlow's sermon was an extraordinary panegyric of his sovereign in terms which made even James' own self-glorification seem rather flat. The King was not only a 'universal scholar, acute in arguing, subtle in distinguishing, logical in discussing', he was also 'a faithful Christian': and so forth and so on, in what has been described as an evocation of the King as 'something of a Christ figure'.[7]

An awareness of having had a narrow escape was not of course confined to the King and Dr Barlow. Queen Anne, that famously fruitful vine, found herself being congratulated all over again on her fecundity in every loyal address. Yet, in her case, once sheer relief − for she would certainly have been present at the Opening − had given way to a more sober consideration of the future, she could appreciate the shadows falling over her Catholicism. As James' Queen Consort, she had attended Protestant services (although without taking the Sacrament); she had agreed to the baptism of the Princess Mary in the Protestant rite in May, while she herself had similarly undergone the ceremony of 'churching' (the purification of a woman after childbirth) in the Protestant rite. At the same time, she maintained her position as a closet Catholic − literally so, since her Mass had to be heard extremely privately in her own apartments.

This graceful ambivalence might not survive in the post-Plot atmosphere of England, and in fact Queen Anne was careful to evade meeting the emissaries of the Catholic powers. She declined to meet Baron Hoboken, envoy of the Archdukes, for two years, thanks to their laggard response to the Hugh Owen business. A convenient fever also caused her to cancel an audience with Zuñiga immediately after the Plot's discovery, lest the Queen's patriotism be suspect. When she did meet the Spaniard, towards the end of November, she spoke at length about her grief at the unfortunate plight of Catholics, and her desire to help them.[8] But in the future her active Catholic sympathies found their expression chiefly in trying to secure grand Catholic marriages for her children.

Another member of the Royal Family who became aware of her own escape as details of the Plot emerged was the nine-year-old Princess Elizabeth. When the alarm came from Warwick, she had been bundled off to Coventry, which was thought to be safer than Coombe Abbey. In her case, she had escaped abduction rather than death, but she made it clear to her guardian Lord Harington that what had been proposed for her by the conspirators would have been a fate *worse* than death. Lord Harington reported: 'Her Highness doth often say "What a Queen should I have been by this means? I had rather been with my Royal Father in the Parliament-house, than wear the Crown on such condition".' Not surprisingly, the shock of it all left the little girl 'very ill and troubled'.[9]

If Queen Anne was justified in bewailing, however ineffectively, the unfortunate plight of the English Catholics, that of the conspirators was infinitely worse. Those at Holbeach – Thomas Wintour, Ambrose Rookwood and John Grant, all in bad physical shape – were taken first to Worcester in the custody of the Sheriff and then to the Tower of London. Meanwhile the bodies of Robert Catesby and Thomas Percy were exhumed from their midland graves by orders of the government, and their heads cut off. The intention was to exhibit the decapitated heads at the corners of the Parliament House which they had planned to blow up. (The blacksmith who forged the ironwork to make this possible was paid 23 shillings and 9 pence.) Among those who inspected these grisly relics *en route* to London was Lord Harington himself, who thought that 'more terrible countenances were never looked upon'. He discerned a special evil mark on their foreheads, a description one suspects that he passed on to his royal charge to fuel her understandable fears still further.*[10]

Thomas Bates, Catesby's servant, was taken prisoner in Staffordshire, and Robert Keyes, who had broken away from the Dunchurch meeting, was also caught. Sir Everard Digby,

---

* This ghoulish practice was not special to the dead Gunpowder Plotters; the heads and limbs of traitors were commonly so displayed; these relics might survive *in situ* for a considerable time as an awful warning of the perils of betraying the state.

who had intended to turn himself in to Sir Fulke Greville at Warwick, was discovered by a small posse of pursuers with two servants concealed in 'a dry pit'. Excited cries of 'Here he is! Here he is!' were met by the imperturbable reply of the gallant horseman: 'Here he is indeed! What then?' Since Digby did not intend to surrender to such small fry, he advanced his horse 'in the manner of curvetting' – that is, in an expert equestrian leap.[11] He would have broken out of the encirclement had he not spied reinforcements of several hundred men coming up behind the posse. He then gave himself up to the most senior-looking man among them. These conspirators, also, were eventually taken to London.

By December, only Robert Wintour, of the surviving comrades, was still at liberty. In London, Francis Tresham was arrested, following Guido's denunciation on 12 November, and taken to the Tower three days later. Three leading Catholic peers, Lord Montague, Lord Mordaunt and Lord Stourton, who all had embarrassing connections to the abortive Plot, were also taken to the Tower. Lord Montague had not only briefly employed Guy Fawkes, but had probably been tipped off by Catesby not to attend Parliament; Lord Mordaunt was Keyes' patron as well as being connected to him by marriage and had planned to be absent because he disliked the coming legislation; Lord Stourton was Tresham's brother-in-law, and Guido had said he would have been detained from the Opening by some kind of accident. The prisoners in the Tower were joined on 27 November by the Earl of Northumberland, transferred from Lambeth.

While plans for the intensive interrogation of the Plotters and their presumed allies were being worked out by the government in London, the English recusant community was suffering exactly that kind of relentless investigation which it had feared for so long. There was now no reason for the authorities to let sleeping recusants – and their priests – lie. On the one hand, further information about the recent wicked conspiracy must be sought, and on the other hand old scores might be paid off (there was always a degree of vindictiveness about the poursuivants' action, nor were they above making a financial profit from it). The desire to make a good thing out of the Powder Treason was not however confined to one rank in society. One of the communications on this subject to Salisbury was that of Susan Countess of Kent who was quite sure – on no particular grounds – that a certain Mr William Willoughby must have been mixed up in the conspiracy. As a result of his presumed villainy, she suggested that she might have his £200 living in Suffolk.[12]

White Webbs, in Enfield Chase, was searched on 11 November and found to have 'many trap doors and passages'. Anne Vaux, alias Mrs Perkins, was of course absent and had been for some time, since Father Garnet judged the house too dangerous a refuge. But four servants were found there: James Johnson, who was about forty, Elizabeth Shepheard, the wife of the coachman, Margaret Walker, in her twenties, who had been in the service of 'Mrs Perkins' for three years, and Jane Robinson, aged fourteen, who was known as the 'Little Girl'. While all admitted to being 'obstinate Papists', they denied at first that the Mass had ever been said at White Webbs.[13]

Then the terrified Jane Robinson gave the game away. She said that there had been a Mass said within the last month but she could remember nothing about the priest except he was 'apparelled like a gentleman'. Father Garnet, the alleged brother of Mrs Perkins, had been known as Mr Meaze there; and yes, in answer to questioning, he had had quite separate apartments from Mrs Perkins. This was probably intended to establish that Mr Meaze was in fact a priest, not a bona-fide brother of Mrs Perkins, whose true identity was not at this point known. But the question marked the beginning of officialdom's prurient interest in the relationship of 'Mr Meaze' and 'Mrs Perkins', which would continue till the day of the former's death, and cause him great pain. James Johnson was now taken up to London and held in the Gatehouse prison.

The long-anticipated search of Harrowden took place over nine days beginning on 12 November. Father Gerard, an unseen, well-hidden presence throughout, was a veteran of such searches, and knew, like all the recusants, the importance of absolute attention to detail. Candles could not even be lit in the kind of dark hole where a priest was concealed, lest the characteristic smell of snuffed-out wax gave the game away. During one search, at Braddocks near Saffron Walden in the 1590s, Gerard had had to exist for four days on two biscuits and a pot of quince jelly which his hostess, Mrs Wiseman, happened to have in her hand as the poursuivants burst in and he was bundled away.

At Harrowden, Gerard was able to sit down but not to stand up in his refuge. But on this occasion he did not starve, since this hiding-place contained one of Little John's characteristic devices, a tube through which he could receive food. After about four days, Eliza Vaux distracted the attention of the authorities by prudently revealing a hiding-place which contained 'many Popish books' and other objects of devotion, 'but no man in it', said the disgruntled government report. The search let up a little after this. Thus Gerard could be brought out at night and warmed by the fire. On 21 November, the searchers finally departed, quite convinced that no one could have survived their inspection.[14] Father Gerard was safe.

By the time the search was abandoned, Eliza Vaux had already been taken away to London under arrest, and had undergone her first interrogation. She was, after all, in deep trouble already with her unfortunate letter to Agnes Lady Wenman and her ill-timed efforts to suborn Sir Richard Verney into releasing her friends. Even her father, Sir John Roper, who was Clerk of the Common Pleas, wrote her an angry letter of remonstrance over her behaviour. Now over seventy, he was determined not to die without acquiring the peerage he believed to be his due. All Roper's succulent presents to Salisbury, including fruit, falcons, game and 'a great standing bowl', were likely to go to waste if his own daughter let the side down by recusancy. And maybe – with the news of this frightful treason – she had let the side down with something worse than that...But Eliza Vaux, as a widow with a cause, was perfectly capable of standing up for herself: as Sir Thomas Tresham and the late Lord Vaux had discovered.

She responded to Sir John with equal indignation. In a letter addressed to 'my loving father' and signed 'your obedient daughter', she craved her father's blessing, but the text between these conventional salutations was anything but submissive. Eliza professed her absolute amazement that her father could for one moment believe that she had had anything to do with the recent conspiracy. As it was, it would be another eleven years and a colossal amount of money expended before Sir John Roper finally got his peerage; he spent the last two years of his life gratifyingly entitled Lord Teynham.[15]

In front of the Council, Eliza Vaux was equally spirited.[16] She refused to admit a number of things. Most importantly, she absolutely refused to give way on the subject of Father Gerard's priesthood. She swore she had not known that Gerard and the others were priests, since they looked 'nothing like priests'; she had taken them for Catholic gentlemen. (This was a vital denial since the penalties for harbouring priests could include death.) She also absolutely refused to admit that Father Gerard had been or was now at Harrowden. She said she had no idea of his whereabouts, but, if she had, she would not give them away to save her own life or anyone else's.

One of the Councillors who had always been friendly to her – probably Northampton – now escorted her courteously to the door. 'Have a little pity on yourself and your children,' he said in a low voice. 'And tell them what they wish to know. If you don't you will have to die.'

But Eliza answered in a loud, bold voice: 'Then I would rather die, my Lord.' Her servants listening outside the door burst into tears. Northampton's words had of course been intended purely to cow her – which they did not succeed in doing – and Eliza Vaux did not die.

She was put into the custody of an alderman, Sir John Swynnerton, in London, and made to remain with him for many months until a plea to Salisbury got her bail. At this point Eliza cunningly manipulated the contemporary image of a female as both frail and indiscreet. How on earth could she have been entrusted with the details of the treason? Who would dream of putting 'their lives and estates in the power and secrecy of a woman'?[17] Her questions were wonderfully disingenuous for someone who had been breaking the law with courage and consistency for years. The truth was that the discovery of Father Gerard (or any other priest) at Harrowden could have destroyed her and her family, but the secret structures of Little John preserved them all. The only inevitable casualty was the match between Edward Lord Vaux and Lady Elizabeth Howard. Within two months, the girl had been married off to a grand old widower, forty years her senior.

Eliza Vaux had handled herself and her secrets well. The wives of the actual conspirators were in far more parlous situation, from which bravery and bluff could not rescue them. Six wives, among other women connected to minor figures in the Plot, were brought up to London, and housed, like Eliza Vaux, by the City aldermen. Martha Wright Percy and Dorothy Wintour Grant, sisters as well as wives of Plotters, were in a specially fraught situation. Then there were Dorothy and Margaret Wright, wives of Jack and Kit, Christiana Keyes, the governess wife of Robert, and Elizabeth Rookwood (Martha Bates does not seem to have been rated worthy of arrest). Notification from the Sheriff to the government following these arrests drew attention to one poignant aspect of the wives' removal to London. He had, he said, 'taken care and charge of these women's children until your honours' pleasures be further known'.[18]

The conspirators' homes were searched and in many cases looted. Goods sought were seized at Ashby St Ledgers, although this was the property of Lady Catesby rather than of her son. Huddington Court was similarly treated. By 17 November, nothing of any real value was said to be left there, since so much had been taken away every day; although some devotional objects and books to do with the Mass were discovered in a hollow in the wall a few weeks later.[19] Even John Talbot, Robert Wintour's staunchly patriotic father-in-law, had his house searched and arms and papers removed. (These papers, not surprisingly, revealed nothing to do with the treason.)

One of the most piteous situations was that of Mary Lady Digby. Brought up as a wealthy young woman, she found that great possessions now made her an outstanding target for rapacity. Gayhurst was ransacked. 'Base people' were everywhere. Even the servants' belongings (which were certainly not forfeit) were simply transported away. The cattle and grain were sold at half price.

As for Mary herself, the Sheriff would not let her have 'apparel' to send to her husband in the Tower, nor for herself 'linens for present wearing about my body' (underwear). In a desperate plea to Salisbury, Mary wrote that the Sheriff – who would probably make over a thousand pounds profit 'underhand' – was dealing in all the properties at Gayhurst 'as though they were absolutely his'. As a result, she was utterly destitute, having nowhere for herself and her children 'to abide in' and nothing for their maintenance. Judging from the official records, it does not seem that Mary Digby exaggerated. The Sheriff himself wrote proudly: 'All goods are carried away, even to the very floor of the great parlour.'[20]

In the Tower of London, that fire and brimstone which had been so miraculously averted from Parliament was being brought down upon the heads of the erstwhile conspirators. Coke afterwards said that the interrogations had taken 'twenty and three several days' altogether (in a ten-week period), with a separate commission set up to examine the lesser folk – not only minor people who had become involved at Dunchurch but serving people and bystanders who could act as witnesses.[21]

The Lieutenant's Lodgings, under the control of Sir William Waad, were used for the important interrogations. Waad, now in his sixties, had been made Lieutenant of the Tower in August. The appointment marked a long career of diplomacy and intrigue in the service of Salisbury's father Burghley, and it was Waad who had first ransacked, then skilfully rearranged the papers of Mary Queen of Scots in 1586. It was also Waad, involved in the discovery of all the major conspiracies of late Elizabethan and early Jacobean times, who was responsible for the interrogations centring on the Main and Bye Plots of 1603. Significantly 'that villain Waad' was later accused by Lord Cobham of tricking him into signing a piece of blank white paper so that Waad could forge his confession. Like Sir Edward Popham, Waad had a vindictive dislike of Catholics beyond the call of duty, and as Clerk of the Privy Council had been ardent in the pursuit of priests and recusants.[22]

In October 1608 he erected a monument to his work on the discovery of the Powder Treason, which ended by quoting, in Hebrew, the Book of Job: 'He discovereth deep things out of darkness, and bringeth out to light the shadow of death.'* Where the Catholics were concerned, bringing deep things out of darkness was certainly the aim of Sir William Waad.

Only two of the 'confessions' which resulted from these numerous interrogations were ever made officially public. These appeared in the so-called *King's Book*, printed for the general edification about the end of November.[23] The *King's Book* had a wide circulation, stimulating popular interest in the recent dramatic – and potentially horrifying – events still further. (Among those stimulated by it may well have been Shakespeare as he worked on his new play, *Macbeth*.) The two statements printed in the *King's Book* were a version of Guy Fawkes' original full confession of 8 November, revised on 17 November, and the confession of Thomas Wintour signed on 23 November. Otherwise, the state papers provide various versions of the numerous interviews, while Coke quoted from them, freely adapted according to the needs of his prosecution, at the coming trials.

* The monument – still extant today – begins with a tribute to King James ('most renowned for piety, justice, prudence, learning, courage, clemency and the other Royal virtues ...'), then names the Councillors who helped uncover the Plot, before listing the Plotters themselves, including Sir William Stanley, Hugh Owen and Father William Baldwin (see plate section). But the Council Chamber where it lies cannot literally have been the site of the interrogations, since it was carved out of the Great Hall only in 1607. (Parnell, *Tower*, p. 61.)

Was torture used once more? There was no further official sanction for torture given this year, other than the King's letter of authorisation concerning Guido and 'the gentler tortures' already quoted. The eager recommendation to Salisbury by Lord Dunfermline, the Lord Chancellor of Scotland, that 'the prisoners should be confined apart, in darkness, and examined by torchlight, and that the tortures be slow and at intervals, as being most effectual', is no proof that Salisbury actually followed his suggestion, although it does indicate the kind of atmosphere then prevailing.* More concrete evidence of the use of torture is provided by a letter from Salisbury himself, dated 4 December. In a document which is difficult to interpret in any other sense, he complained of the conspirators' obstinate refusal to incriminate the priests, 'yea, what torture soever they be put to'.[24]

It suggests that some at least of the Plotters had been subject to the manacles, or perhaps they had simply been shown the rack to terrify them: a method of interrogation which could be construed as needing no authorisation. The same technique may have been used over the trial of Ralegh. Coke denied that a certain witness had been threatened with the rack, answering smoothly: 'we told him he deserved the Rack, but did not threaten him with it'.[25] Since Salisbury and the government were now trying to entrap men who were innocent – the priests – in the same net as the guilty – the conspirators – they were no longer engaged in simply laying bare the truth. In order to achieve false or partially false confessions, torture and its threat might indeed be necessary.

A candidate for torture may have been the young recusant Henry Huddlestone, who made a series of confessions about that fatal meeting on the road with Catesby, and his expedition thereafter with the priests. Father Strange, captured with him, was certainly tortured at some point ('grievously racked'), although probably not until the next wave of interrogations in 1606.[26]

---

* As for King James' personal attitude to torture, it should be borne in mind, given his Scottish Lord Chancellor's words, that the practice certainly did not come to him as an English novelty; he had grown up with its use.

Yet the first confessions, those of November, did not provide that precise, strong link between the priests and the Plot which would have been convenient for the government. In his declaration of 13 November (the day after his arrest) Francis Tresham, while generally exculpating himself, did implicate Father Garnet in the abortive negotiations with Spain of 1602 – the so-called Spanish Treason.[27] This was helpful so far as it went, because the Spanish Treason was otherwise a somewhat tricky subject for the government to handle. It was undoubtedly a treasonable venture, whether described by Wintour or Guy Fawkes, for it was certainly treason to seek the armed assistance of a foreign power in order to overthrow the existing government of England. However, times had changed and there was absolutely no advantage, and a great deal of possible disadvantage, in berating the Spanish King in the new warm climate following the Anglo-Spanish Treaty. To make the Spanish Treason a Jesuit-inspired enterprise was the tactful solution.

In exactly the same way, the government were concerned to impose the names of their enemies Hugh Owen, Sir William Stanley and Father William Baldwin upon the conspiracy. Since the Plot already contained quite enough genuinely treasonable material, this imposition was for their own wider purposes. It has been noted that Salisbury had been quick off the mark in demanding the extradition of the detested Owen from the Spanish Netherlands. In the two published confessions of Guido and Tom Wintour, if collated with the various drafts and versions still in existence, there is evidence that these names were deliberately introduced. Salisbury let himself go about 'that creature Owen' in a letter to Sir Thomas Edmondes of 2 December. He instructed the Ambassador in Brussels carefully on the version of the Plot which must be spread among Owen's friends. It should be 'as evident as the sun in the clearest day' that Stanley, Father Baldwin and Owen were all involved 'in this matter of the gunpowder'. Furthermore, Baldwin, via Owen, and 'Owen directly of himself' had been 'particular conspirators'.[28]

In short, a Cold War was being conducted (and had long been conducted) with the Catholic intriguers across the water. This meant that matters of veracity were less important than the wider issue of ensuring Protestant success.

Tom Wintour's confession was supposedly signed by him on 23 November. He added to it further details of the so-called Spanish Treason on 26 November.[29] Wintour's account became the basis for most other subsequent narratives, including that of Father Tesimond himself. This was not only because the confession was published at length, but also because Wintour, uniquely among the survivors, had been in on the Powder Treason since the beginning. Guido, battered and tortured as he might be, could still not provide the full details of those early days with Catesby, the season before he himself was recruited.

It is, however, a document which cannot be taken purely at its face value. This is because Wintour's signature at the bottom – 'Thomas Winter' (sic) – is quite impossible to reconcile with any signature that had been made by him in the past. The version 'Wintour' was the one invariably used by him – whereas the version 'Winter' (or 'Wynter') was generally used by the government.[30] There is a further difficulty posed by the signature, which, whatever its spelling, is not noticeably shaky. Yet this was the alleged signature of a man who had been seriously wounded in the shoulder, losing the use of his right arm, less than a fortnight previously. Nor does Waad's report to Salisbury on 21 November inspire confidence: 'Winter' (sic) now found his hand so strong that he would write down after dinner what he had already declared to Salisbury verbally; the prisoner would then add 'what he shall further remember'. The implication is that Tom Wintour by now was remembering what he was told to remember.[31]

Wintour, since his confession was so vital, may well have been exposed to the awesome sight of the rack. But perhaps, wounded and helpless as he was, it was not necessary. The implicit threat of his situation – the despair of the prisoner cut off in the darkness described by Lord Dunfermline – may have been enough for the government to produce from him the confession they wanted. At all events, a surviving draft marked in Coke's handwriting shows how carefully the text was monitored: wording has been altered in places, and underlined in others. The main drift of these markings is to hammer home the involvement of the Jesuits, especially Gerard, and of course the guilt of Owen.[32]

Then there was the question of the famous mine under the House of Lords, which had not been mentioned in Guido's first confession, but featured, by a strange coincidence, in both the confessions which were published. It was suggested earlier that this mine – for which no independent corroboration exists and of which no trace remains – was a myth promulgated by the government. Its importance in the *King's Book* was as an artistic effect intended to emphasise the sheer horror of what had happened – or rather, what had nearly happened. Having elaborated the kind of confession they wanted from Wintour – both for evidence and for publication purposes – it is scarcely surprising that the government then went further and appended his signature to it. Wintour was completely in their power: the forged signature – by 'that villain Waad' yet again? – was only the culmination of the process.

If the Council had not got all the information it wanted about the priests, it had also not succeeded in probing that worrying matter of the future Protector's identity. The Earl of Northumberland was not, of course, tortured or even threatened with torture. He was a great man, not an obscure recusant. He was, however, subjected to intensive questioning by the King among others. James was preoccupied with the idea that Northumberland had had his horoscope – and that of the royal children – drawn up: casting the horoscope of a reigning monarch was always seen as a threatening and thus treasonable activity. Northumberland's problem, as he himself would point out to the King a few years later, was that he could not prove a negative. On 15 November, in front of the Council, he had argued that he should be presumed innocent on the grounds of

his lifestyle, which was 'unambitious and given to private pleasures, such as gardening and building'.[33] Unfortunately this
touching picture was not the whole image of the man.

It was Northumberland who had acted as the Catholics'
advocate in the previous reign, something the Earl might loftily
dismiss as 'an old Scotch story', but others did not forget so
easily. It was Northumberland who had employed Thomas
Percy (a dead man who could tell no tales, even to exonerate
his patron) and it was Northumberland who had been visited
by Percy at Syon on 4 November, before the latter went back
to Essex House, Northumberland's London home. Against
this, Northumberland, denying over and over again any complicity in the Plot, could only point to the practical arrangements he had made to attend Parliament on 5 November.
Even Salisbury admitted to Edmondes: 'it cannot be cast
[charged] that he was absent'.[34]

It was not enough. Northumberland remained in the Tower,
although he lived in comfort compared to the prisoners in
their dungeons below.[35] Nevertheless he was not a free man.
Assuming that he was innocent, Northumberland, like the
Plotters' wives, was among the numerous tangential victims of
the Powder Treason.

The rest of the prisoners held in connection with the Plot –
with one key exception – did not provide the government with
anything very much in the way of fresh information. Men like
Ambrose Rookwood and Sir Everard Digby had been brought
into the conspiracy too late to have much detailed knowledge.*
Rookwood's main contribution beyond attesting to his enduring feelings for Catesby, whom he 'loved more than his own
soul', was to state that he had been promised that the Catholic
lords would be spared.†[36]

---

* The fact that the majority of the principal Plotters – Catesby, Percy and the
Wright brothers – died at Holbeach House on 8 November meant that their
version of the conspiracy would never be known; this complicated its unravelling
for the government in 1605, and has continued to complicate it for historians
ever since.
† There is the etched name 'Ambrose Rookwoode' still to be seen in the upper
Martin Tower (R.C.H., p. 83b (no. 12)).

As for Digby, he suffered from the delusion, pathetic under the circumstances, that he could explain everything to King James if only he could meet him face to face, and put the Catholic case.[37] Of course the once petted darling of the court was not allowed this luxury. One can hardly blame King James for not wishing to entertain further a young man who had recently planned to murder him and his family in such a ruthless fashion. Nevertheless Digby's conduct either raises a doubt about the full extent of his implication, or suggests that Digby was astonishingly naive and trusting of his sovereign's forgiveness.

Digby had been involved in the conspiracy a mere fortnight before its discovery. It is possible that he learnt the full dreadful nature of what had been planned for the Parliament House only at Dunchurch when the London conspirators arrived to disband the meeting, by which time the Plot had already failed. Digby was not the kind of man to desert his friends at this juncture, and so he pressed on with them (although his reaction to the servant at the inn – 'there is no remedy' – suggests he did so with a heavy heart). But he did of course leave Holbeach, when the cause was evidently lost, to surrender himself to the authorities, and he was the only major conspirator to do so.

Denied an interview with the King, Digby took refuge in a kind of Christian defiance, as family papers discovered after his son's death revealed. 'If I had thought there had been the least sin in the Plot,' he wrote, 'I would not have been of it for all the world, and no other cause drew me to hazard my life but zeal to God's religion.' As for the reaction of the Pope and the English priesthood, he had been assured that they would not hinder any 'stirs' (risings) that should be undertaken 'for the Catholic good'.[38] Apart from writing, he occupied himself, like Rookwood, with carving an inscription in his cell at the Broad Arrow Tower.*

---

* This inscription is still extant, although it is currently (1996) covered by a panel to allow for an exhibition connected to the Peasants' Revolt of 1381 (R.C.H., p. 82b (no. 15); information to the author from Yeoman Warder B. Harrison.).

The key confession which forged the link between priests and Plot so much desired by Salisbury was that of Thomas Bates on 4 December.[39] This confession constituted something of a breakthrough, because Bates directly implicated Father Tesimond (something he would apologise for at the last). This false witness was born almost certainly as a result of his being threatened with torture on the one hand and promised a pardon on the other: that is certainly what Father Tesimond himself believed, accepting in effect Bates' ultimate apology. But by then it was of course too late to save the Powder Treason from its transformation into the Case of the Conspiring Jesuits.

Bates, unfortunately, was in all too good a position to give the kind of testimony which would be lethal in the hands of an agile prosecutor. In his capacity as Catesby's servant, he had been present at so many of the crucial scenes of the conspiracy. His great loyalty had been to his master, but now Catesby was dead, and he at least was beyond the government's vengeance. Thus, in a subsequent examination of 13 January 1606, Bates was able to describe the mission he had made to Father Garnet at Coughton on 7 November, on Catesby's instructions, to break the devastating news of the Plotters' flight. He could report the fatal exchange between the two priests, Father Garnet and Father Tesimond, and that exclamation – all too accurate, as it turned out – 'we are all undone!' It was Bates who had ridden with Father Tesimond to Huddington, before Tesimond went to the Habingtons at Hindlip. Bates also spoke of a meeting between three priests, Garnet, Gerard and Tesimond, at Harrowden, some time in mid-October.[40]

Putting Bates' testimony with that of Francis Tresham on 29 November which linked Father Garnet with the earlier Spanish Treason of 1602, Salisbury was rapidly developing the case he wanted against the Jesuits, one which specifically connected them to the recent treason. (As Catholic priests, their presence in England was of course already contrary to the law.)

Then in December there was an unexpected complication.
Francis Tresham, held in the Tower of London, went into a
rapid physical decline. The condition he was suffering from,
known as strangury, was caused by an acute and painful
inflammation of the urinary tract. This was no sudden out-of-
the-blue attack. The condition had evidently been with
Tresham some time before the current crisis, since he already
had a doctor in charge of him. This was a distinguished man,
Dr Richard Foster, who had recently been President of the
College of Physicians. Tresham preferred him to the regular
Tower doctor, Dr Matthew Gwinne, because Foster knew all
about his case.[41]

By mid-December Tresham was being described by Sir
William Waad as 'worse and worse'. Indeed, Waad wondered
gloomily whether Tresham would survive long enough to meet
the death he deserved. In addition to Foster, three more
doctors were being called, and a woman – a nurse – was also
admitted to attend him. Tresham already had his own man in
attendance, one William Vavasour, who acted more as a confi-
dential assistant than as a servant, as was Thomas Bates to
Robert Catesby. Vavasour was supposed to be an illegitimate
son of the late philoprogenitive Sir Thomas, and thus Francis
Tresham's half-brother.[42] This would have made sense of their
intimacy by the standards of the time, when the 'base born'
were often provided with just this kind of family employment.
(Rumours that Thomas Percy was an illegitimate half-brother
of Northumberland were in fact untrue, but demonstrate how
frequently contemporary patronage had its roots in this kind of
relationship.)

While Waad squabbled pettishly with the Lord Mayor of
London about who was in charge of what (the latter had the
irksome habit of parading about 'the greatest part of the
Tower' with a ceremonial sword carried in front of him to
assert his authority), Francis Tresham groaned in his cell. Anne
Tresham, another gallantly supportive wife, joined him two
days before the end came. But it was in fact left to Vavasour
to take down Francis Tresham's deathbed confession, since

Anne was by this time too upset. Vavasour also wrote an affecting account of his master's last hours.*[43]

Tresham died slowly, agonisingly and inexorably. This wayward, treacherous and perhaps ultimately self-hating character was however, like many such, intending to do better in the next world than in the one he would shortly leave. Above all, he wanted to make restitution to Father Garnet for implicating him in the Spanish Treason of 1602. In the statement he dictated to Vavasour – 'because he could not write himself, being so weak' – Tresham referred to Garnet (under the name of Mr Whalley) as someone whose safety he respected and tendered as much as his own, adding 'many words' on 'the virtues and worthiness of the man'. Tresham desired that his former confession might be called in and that 'this [new one] may stand for truth'. He then pledged 'his Salvation' that he had in fact no idea whether Tom Wintour had had any letter of recommendation from Garnet for his visit to Spain 'about the latter end of the Queen's days ... for he did not see Mr Whalley [Garnet] at that time, nor had seen him in fifteen or sixteen year before ...'.[44]

This was a vital piece of exculpation – how vital would not be totally clear, of course, so long as Father Garnet remained securely in hiding. (He had gone to ground at Hindlip at the beginning of December.) It is, though, proof that Tresham, even as he was dying, understood the value of what he had said and that he specifically commanded a copy of the document to be got to Garnet even before it reached Salisbury. As Vavasour wrote: this was 'my Master's special desire'. But it did not happen. Anne Tresham was prostrate with grief after her husband's death, and in her own words 'altogether unfit', while Vavasour himself was held prisoner.[45] So Garnet was never to know exactly what Tresham had said. The omission is

* This account by Vavasour is of special importance since it lay for three hundred years unknown to, and thus untouched by, the government – among the muniments at Deene Park, the home of Thomas Brudenell; he had married one of Francis' numerous sisters, Mary, in the summer of 1605 and would assist his mother-in-law Muriel Lady Tresham in her administrative duties after Francis' death, so the document's presence at Deene makes sense (Wake, p. 31).

understandable, given the desperate circumstances in which they were all living; but in this world of governmental manipulation such a failure of communication was to prove extremely dangerous.

The rest of Tresham's deathbed confession repeated the protestations of virtual ignorance and thus practical innocence which had occupied him on 13 November. He had, after all, his two little daughters' future to protect. He commended Lucy and Eliza to his brother Lewis as Christ had commended his mother to St John. He never, however, referred to the Monteagle Letter at any point, which makes it virtually certain that Tresham did not write it. He would hardly have failed to claim the credit for it at a time when Monteagle, for his contribution, was being hailed as the saviour of his country.

When Tresham refused to add to his statement, in answer to the questions of the hovering Waad, saying that he had nothing heavy on his conscience, the Lieutenant of the Tower went away angry. Significantly, the son's obsession with the father continued to the last. Francis observed, as he read *De Imitatione Christi*, that he hoped to make a better death than old Sir Thomas, who had died tossing and turning only three months before.

Francis Tresham did make a holy death: if not the short half-hour of agony which he had wished for himself.[46] The Litany and Prayer of the Virgin Mary and St John were said around his bedside by Anne Tresham and William Vavasour as Francis gradually became too weak to join in. Vavasour was asked to remind him to call upon the Name of Jesus (a Catholic devotion) at ten o'clock, but when Vavasour went to wake him Tresham looked 'ghastly', did not recognise Vavasour and tried to shake him off. About midnight, more Litanies, the Confiteor and the Mea Culpa were recited; at two o'clock in the morning on 23 December, Francis Tresham died.

Thereafter the government tried to treat the dead man as a traitor, despite the fact that he had never been indicted as such, in order to confiscate Tresham's goods and lands, along with those of the other conspirators. Ironically enough, the entail in the male line made by Sir Thomas in 1584, which had proved such a burden to Francis in his lifetime, now turned out to be a blessing in disguise, as did the fact that Francis left only daughters. Since Francis Tresham proved to be a mere life tenant in much of the estate, a great deal of it was able to pass to his brother Lewis. As for his mortal remains, we must assume that Francis Tresham, like Catesby and Percy, was indifferent to the fact that his decapitated head was posted up in Northampton, since he died, by government standards, impenitent. His headless body was tumbled into 'a hole' on Tower Hill.[47]

Unfortunately, Francis Tresham left a further legacy, one which would justify the words of Shakespeare in *Julius Caesar*, a play first performed about five years earlier:

> The evil that men do lives after them,
> The good is oft interred with their bones...

CHAPTER FOURTEEN

These Wretches

~~~~~~~~~

[The Powder Treason] shameth Caligula, Erostratus,
Nero and Domitian, who were but each of them fly-
killers to these wretches.

LORD HARINGTON
6 January 1606

In the new year of 1606, the popular mood concerning the recent Powder Treason was one of mingled revulsion and relief, but also that secret delight which the contemplation of horrors narrowly averted inevitably produces. The opening of a poem appearing on 3 January, entitled *The Devil of the Vault*, captures this particular mood of gleeful shuddering:*

> So dreadful, foul, chimera-like
> My subject must appear:
> The Heaven amaz'd and hell disturbed
> The earth shall quake with fear.[1]

But the King himself was not gleeful: he was sour and angry. The courage and statesmanship he had shown in his speech to Parliament of 9 November had given way to something a good deal less attractive and a good deal more vengeful. With time, the memory of his kindnesses to the Catholics – the ungrateful Catholics – was beginning to loom large in his

---

* The phrase 'Devil of the Vault', which took a hold on the popular imagination, was originally used by Bishop Barlow in his sermon of 10 November (Nowak, p. 41).

own mind, while the important distinction between the guilty and the innocent Papists was beginning to blur. To the Venetian Ambassador, Niccolò Molin, he ranted for an hour on the subject of 'this perfidious and cursed doctrine of Rome' which produced English subjects who believed they could plot against their lawful Prince. James told Molin that the Catholics threatened to 'dethrone him and take his life' unless he gave them liberty of conscience. In consequence of their behaviour: 'I shall, most certainly, be obliged to stain my hands with their blood,' although, with his reputation as a merciful sovereign to maintain, he added: 'sorely against my will.'[2]

The blood with which the government was hoping to stain the King's hands – in addition to that of the Plotters – was Jesuit blood. By 15 January, it was decided that enough material had been accrued to proceed against certain priests. The official proclamation listed Father Garnet, Father Gerard and Father Greenway (Tesimond) and issued the usual meticulous descriptions employed in these circumstances. Father Garnet, for example, was said to be a man 'of middling stature, full faced, fat of body, of complexion fair, his forehead high on each side, with a little thin hair coming down ... the hair of his head and beard grizzled'. His age was reckoned to be between fifty and sixty (life in hiding had aged Father Garnet: born late in 1555, he was only just fifty). At least his gait was said to be 'upright and comely' for a man who was so weak.[3] This proclamation marked a radical and ironic shift in the direction of the prosecution. From now on, with tragic irony, the names of the Jesuits headed the list of conspirators in the Plot which they had so desperately attempted to circumvent.

In London, Father Tesimond had the unnerving experience of reading details of his 'good red complexion' and his tendency to wear showy clothes 'after the Italian fashion' when the proclamation was posted up. Then the priest's eyes met those of a man in the crowd and he realised that his appearance was being checked out. When the stranger suggested that they go together to the authorities, Tesimond with seeming docility allowed himself to be led away, until they reached a quiet street, where the priest took to his heels and ran off. Tesimond then rapidly and discreetly left London, managing to smuggle aboard a cargo of dead pigs headed for Calais. From there he went to St Omer and finally on to Rome. Here a long and comparatively happy life awaited him: Father Tesimond survived for another thirty years after these tumultuous events. Most importantly he was one of those who lived to tell the tale from the Catholic angle.[4]

The escape of Father Tesimond was one ray of light in the rapidly encircling gloom of the Catholic situation. On 9 January, two months after their flight from Holbeach, Robert Wintour and Stephen Littleton were captured. It had been a time of great hardship, as well as fear, for these fugitives, who had to camp out in barns, or at best in poor men's houses, in midwinter. They were discovered in one hiding-place, in the outbuildings belonging to a tenant farmer of Humphrey Littleton, by a drunken poacher whom they had to imprison in order to make their escape. Since New Year's Day they had holed up at Hagley, the Worcestershire house where 'Red Humphrey' Littleton lived with his widowed sister-in-law Mrs Muriel Littleton. The treachery of a cook, John Finwood, led to the fugitives' arrest: the man suspected the extraordinary amount of food being sent up for his mistress's consumption. It was a feat for which Finwood would be rewarded with an annual pension.[5]

When the authorities arrived, Red Humphrey, who was not personally being sought by the government, since he had left Dunchurch without joining the conspirators, tried to prevent their entrance. Fatally for his own cause, he denied the presence of Wintour or his nephew. Another servant, David Bate, knew better and led the searchers round to the back door. Wintour and Stephen Littleton were captured in the adjoining courtyard. Humphrey Littleton then jumped on his gelding and rode away; he had got as far as Prestwood in Staffordshire, before he was seized.

Red Humphrey was imprisoned first at Stafford, and then at Worcester, where he was condemned to death. At this point, his morale collapsed – not all the recusants were heroes. He 'offered to do good service' if his execution might be reprieved. Father Tesimond later commented contemptuously on Littleton's behaviour: here was a man 'who had no further hope of life but was desperately anxious to save it'.[6] Tesimond's contempt is understandable, for Red Humphrey's testimony played its part in the last act of the drama currently being enacted, not far away from Worcester, at Hindlip. Here Father Garnet, together with two lay brothers, Little John and Ralph Ashley, had retreated at the beginning of December. Father Oldcorne, the regular chaplain there, better known under his alias of Hall, was also in residence.

Hindlip was traditionally one of the safest Catholic houses, in spite of the known recusancy of Thomas Habington, himself a convicted conspirator in the previous reign. Like Coughton, it occupied a good position, with views of the surrounding countryside. In addition, it had been custom built by Habington's father in the middle of the last century, to act as a labyrinth of refuges when necessary. (It was infinitely easier to construct these holes and secret closets at the start because there were no tell-tale signs of renovation – sawdust, brick-dust, fresh plaster – to be detected.) An early-nineteenth-century description of Hindlip referred to 'its every room' as having 'a recess, a passage, a trap door, or secret stairs; the walls were in many places false. Several chimneys had double flues, one for a passage for the smoke, the second for the concealment of a priest.'*[7]

All in all, there were at least a dozen hiding-places in use at Hindlip by this date. A search was always a game of cat and mouse. Father Garnet's decision to desert Coughton for Hindlip was based on the premise that at Hindlip the cat might

---

* Hindlip House burnt down shortly after this description was written and was totally rebuilt. No trace of its exotic unlawful past remains: its reincarnation has in fact brought it strictly within the law, for it is now the Headquarters of the West Mercia Police Authority. However, the Church of St James, close by, contains a fine and colourful memorial to the Habington family of Hindlip, including coats of arms.

suspect that there were mice to be found, but could not place the precise whereabouts of the mouseholes.

It was 'at break of day' on Monday 20 January that a local Justice, Sir Henry Bromley, and his retainers arrived outside the house. Sir Henry was the eldest son of Sir Thomas Bromley, who as Lord Chancellor had presided over the trial of Mary Queen of Scots. Yet Muriel Littleton, one of his many sisters, was a recusant, which illustrates the remarkable mixture of religious loyalties which any large family could show at this period. Sir Henry carried with him a commission from the Privy Council. The promise of a 'bountiful reward' for the capture of the miscreant priests meant that he and his men set about the task with enthusiasm. He also had detailed practical instructions on how the search was to be conducted, from the use of a gimlet to pierce panelled walls, to the inspection of any lofts under the roof, 'for these be ordinary places of *hovering*'.[8]

As it happened, Thomas Habington was absent from Hindlip on business when Bromley arrived. When, on his return, Habington was shown the official proclamation for the arrest of the three Jesuits, and Bromley's commission, he strongly and passionately denied the presence of the priests. Indeed, he volunteered to die there and then at his own gate if any Catholic priests were to be found lurking under his roof. This 'rather rash' speech cut no ice with Sir Henry.[9] So for the next three days the most thorough search possible was mounted, regardless of the family's protests.

In this way, a series of hiding-places was uncovered, including two cavities in the brickwork in the gallery over the gate, and three others in the chimneys, where planks of wood had been darkened with soot to match the brick. Altogether eleven 'secret corners and conveyances' were probed, all of them containing 'Popish trumpery' – vessels and books necessary to the celebration of the Mass – except for two which had been uncovered at an earlier date and thus left empty. Thomas Habington, with admirable sang-froid, continued to maintain his stance of absolute ignorance. The revelation of each hiding-place in turn was greeted by him with great surprise. It was only when the vital title deeds to his lands were discovered lodged in one hole for safe-keeping – which might argue for a certain degree of knowledge on the owner's part – that Habington had to waver in his denials.[10]

Then on Thursday morning 24 January there was a break-through of sorts, or so Sir Henry hoped. Two stealthy figures emerged from the wainscot in the gallery. The figures were in fact Nicholas Owen and his fellow lay brother Ralph Ashley and they were starving, having had nothing but one apple between them to eat since the search began on Monday. (Before that, lying in 'a lower chamber descending from the dining-room', they had been able to get food.)[11] It is possible that Owen and Ashley intended to give themselves up, to distract attention from the presence of their superiors Garnet and Oldcorne, concealed elsewhere. But it seems more likely that the two men were attempting to make a bold getaway, choosing a moment when the gallery was, as they thought, empty. Little John in particular knew that, if he were tortured a second time and were compelled to reveal the secrets of his clandestine profession, he would bring ruin not only upon himself, but also upon the entire recusant community.

Unfortunately one of the searchers turned back into the gallery and saw these unexpected strangers. Even now, Owen and Ashley attempted to bluff their way out by pretending to be mere recusants, rather than lay brothers. As for Sir Henry, in his report to Salisbury of the same day, he huffed and puffed about the impudence of the Catholics and their wicked lies, as though the host who hid the priests should have immediately revealed their whereabouts. He then expressed the proud hope that he had found Tesimond (Greenway) and Oldcorne (Hall).[12]

But of course Sir Henry had not found them. When this became apparent, the search was renewed. Bromley did attempt to evacuate the lady of the house, Mary Habington – sister to Monteagle, the hero of the hour – as her presence was obviously awkward for him. But Mary defiantly refused to leave 'without I should have carried her', and Bromley thought this would be conduct unbecoming towards one 'so well born'. On Friday, Saturday and Sunday, the searchers were as rampant as ever, calling to mind Anne Vaux's description of an earlier search at Baddesley Clinton in the 1590s: 'the poursuiv-ants behaved just like a lot of boys playing Blind Man's Bluff, who, in their wild rush, bang into tables and chairs and walls and yet haven't the slightest suspicion that their playfellows are right on top of them and almost touching them'.[13]

It was on the Sunday, 26 January, that Humphrey Littleton, prisoner in nearby Worcester, decided to save his neck – as he hoped. The 'good service' which he offered to do was to betray the names and hiding-place of 'certain Jesuits and priests, which had been persuaders of him and others to these actions'. Hindlip was described as a haunt of priests in general and of Father Hall (Oldcorne) in particular. In addition, Littleton said he was quite sure that Hall was 'in Habington's house at this present', while Hall's own servant, currently in Worcester jail, 'can, he thinks, go directly to the secret places where Hall lies hid'. Littleton backed up these topographical details with a highly damaging account of a conversation he had had with Oldcorne.[14]

Littleton said that he had recently visited 'Father Hall' to consult him about the future of his nephew Stephen. Was it his, Humphrey's, duty to arrest him? According to Littleton, Oldcorne replied that on the contrary the Powder Treason itself had been 'commendable' and that it should not be in any way measured by its lack of success. This was just what the govern-ment wanted to hear – a Jesuit priest openly approving of the Plot. These promising confidences caused the Sheriff of Worcester to stay Littleton's execution, to see if he remembered anything else.

It transpired later that what Father Oldcorne had actually said was somewhat different. On the Plot's lack of success, he cited the instance of Louis XI of France, who had made a pil-grimage to the Holy Land, directed by St Bernard of Clairvaux. Plague had twice struck the King's camp, decimating his men the first time and killing the King himself the second, while his enemies went untouched. Nevertheless these disasters did not necessarily reflect upon the validity of the expedition. In short, an act was 'not to be condemned or justified' by the criterion of its success or failure but, rather, according to its objective and 'the means that is used for effecting the same'. Since Father Oldcorne knew nothing of Catesby's objectives, nor yet of his means, he declared himself as neither approving nor condemning the recent disastrous enterprise: he was content to leave it 'to God and their consciences'.[15] Given that Humphrey Littleton had been wondering whether to hand over his own nephew to the authorities, this was sensible and humane rather than bloodthirsty advice. But of course it could and would be twisted into a very different shape.

Ironically enough, Red Humphrey's treachery may not have been, strictly speaking, the key factor in the apprehension of Fathers Garnet and Oldcorne at Hindlip. On Monday 27 January, the two men emerged of their own accord, looking so like ghosts after an eight-day sojourn in a tiny cramped space that it was their pursuers who were the terrified ones and at first ran away from them. According to Garnet's own account, they had spent most of their time sitting as the hole was not high enough for them to stand up to their full height, nor long enough for them to stretch their legs completely. As a result, their legs, especially those of Father Garnet, were terribly swollen.[16]

The physical ordeal as the two priests listened to the searchers overhead had not been pleasant. It was true that they had been able to receive warm drinks through a quill or reed inserted into a narrow aperture which passed through one chimney – a typical Little John touch – into another chimney in 'the gentlewoman's chamber'. This chamber probably belonged to Anne Vaux, and she would have administered the liquids, including caudle, a sweet spicy kind of gruel especially designed for invalids, through the reed. Marmalade and sweetmeats, staples of this kind of siege, were found in their hole afterwards and must have been brought in with them by the priests themselves. But there was no drainage or earth closet (Little John sometimes managed to effect this – as at Sawston – but had not been able to do so in this particular hiding-place).

That was the trouble. Father Garnet said later that if only they had had half a day of freedom, they could have secured 'a close-stool' (commode). With the aid of that, they could have lasted for another three months. So it was what Sir Henry Bromley would call 'those customs of nature which must of necessity be done' that finally drove out the two priests. Even their captors blanched at the conditions which they found.[17]

Yet before we acquit Humphrey Littleton of all practical contribution to the arrest (morally his culpability remains the same) it must be remembered how long the search had already lasted without the result that the government really wanted. Bromley suspected that there were further priests to be discovered, but he was not absolutely sure – they could have escaped before 20 January. Without further information, Bromley might have given up just a moment before the priests themselves decided to surrender. Humphrey Littleton's Sunday revelations, however, clinched the matter. When the message came to Hindlip – only four miles from Worcester where Littleton was held – Bromley knew that sooner or later the prey would be his. On the Monday, Father Garnet and Father Oldcorne, emaciated and wretched, stepped out into his eager arms.

Garnet and Oldcorne were taken to Sir Henry Bromley's home at Holt Castle until further orders concerning their fate were received from London. They were neither shackled, nor held in collars, nor in any other way treated brutally. Although the whole basis of the official proclamation was that the Jesuits had been the prime persuaders in the recent devilish Plot, their treatment was in no sense that normally meted out to desperadoes. There was a paradox here. Sir Henry Bromley told Garnet that although the proclamation meant that he had to hold him 'strait' yet he honoured him as 'a learned man and a worthy priest'.[18]

In London, Parliament had reassembled on Tuesday 21

January; it had not met since that Saturday in November when the King had made his celebrated speech. In the Commons one of the first actions was to consider measures of safety, with reference to 'the Danger of Papistical Practices'. Two days later Sir Edward Montague, the Member for Northamptonshire, introduced a bill, drafted by himself, for a public thanksgiving to be said annually on 5 November. Sir Edward was often thought to be numbered among the Puritans, being 'a man of plain and downright English spirit'.[19] He was eager to be reinstated in the King's favour after delivering a petition against the suspension of non-conforming clergy which had annoyed James. The Papists' disgrace provided a perfect opening. Montague now introduced the concept of a plain and downright English festival which survived in one form or another for nearly four hundred years.

A more immediate festivity – of a sort – awaited the curious, many months before 5 November 1606. On Monday 27 January, the day of the capture of Father Garnet and Father Oldcorne, the trial of the eight surviving conspirators began in Westminster Hall. Seven of them were brought by barge from the Tower of London to Whitehall, early in the morning: these were Guy Fawkes, Thomas and Robert Wintour, John Grant, Ambrose Rookwood, Everard Digby and Robert Keyes. Thomas Bates' inferior status was marked by the fact that he was held in the less important Gatehouse prison. So 'these wretches', compared to whom villains of the Ancient World such as Nero and Caligula were said to be mere 'fly-killers', prepared to face judgement.[20]

The decision was never in doubt. The mere fact that these men were on trial for high treason meant that they would inevitably be found guilty, and equally inevitably sentenced to death. Refinements such as defending counsel were unknown. In the nineteenth century, Lord Macaulay would describe the process as 'merely a murder preceded by the uttering of certain gibberish and the performance of certain mummeries'. Yet one should be wary of too much anachronistic indignation. These were the rules of a treason trial at the time, proceedings which were quite literally intended as a show trial, one where the guilt of the prisoners would be demonstrated publicly. For this reason, the government encouraged popular attendance at such events. The real trial had already taken place in the form of interrogations before the Privy Council. It was here that guilt or otherwise was decided, since guilt was not a foregone conclusion at this point. Not every prisoner brought before the Privy Council as a suspect traitor was sent for trial.[21]

The prisoners were kept together in the Star Chamber for a short while before being brought into Westminster Hall. Here they were displayed on a scaffold which had been specially devised, and subjected to the fascinated scrutiny of the spectators. These included some secret watchers as well as many members of both Houses of Parliament. (There was a complaint the next day that MPs had been jostled and their reserved places 'pestered with others not of the House'; a committee was set up to investigate.) Among the secret watchers was the King himself, who occupied a room where he could see without being seen. He was said to have been present from eight in the morning until seven at night. Queen Anne and Prince Henry, not quite twelve years old – two potential victims of the Plot – were concealed in another secluded watch-post. Two private rooms were also erected so that foreign ambassadors and other notables could attend the trial discreetly.[22]

As for what they saw, a contemporary description conveys the sense of horrified wonder at the sight of the eight murderous 'wretches'. Some hung down their heads 'as if their hearts were full of doggedness', while others forced 'a stern look, as if they would frighten death with a frown'. None of them gave the impression of praying 'except it were by the dozen upon their beads'. (The Plotters were actually saying the rosary, a Catholic form of prayer much scorned by Protestants, beads being among the devotional objects which were unlawful.) One particular detail must have maddened King James. It was noticed throughout the trial that the conspirators were 'taking tobacco, as if hanging were no trouble to them'. Yet only in

1604 the King had energetically denounced smoking – 'a custom loathsome to the eye, hateful to the nose, harmful to the brain, dangerous to the lungs' – in his *Counterblaste to Tobacco*.²³ The conspirators' addiction was yet another proof of their moral obloquy.

The Lords Commissioners who sat in trial consisted of the Earls of Suffolk, Worcester, Northampton and Devonshire, as well as Salisbury, Sir John Popham as Lord Chief Justice, Sir Thomas Fleming as Lord Chief Baron of the Exchequer and two Justices of the Common Pleas, Sir Thomas Walmsley and Sir Peter Warburton. Of the peers, Worcester had been considered a Papist in the previous reign, and Northampton a Church Papist, but men of Catholic sympathies were of course specially keen to demonstrate their horror of the Powder Treason. Seven of the conspirators – Sir Everard Digby was the exception – were tried on the same indictment.*²⁴

This list of 'false traitors' to the King began, significantly, with the names and common aliases of the three Jesuits, Garnet, Tesimond and Gerard, who were described as 'not yet taken' since the morning's dramatic news had not reached London. The list then passed on to Thomas Wintour, followed by Guido Fawkes, 'otherwise called Guido Johnson', Robert Keyes and Thomas Bates, 'yeoman'. The names of the four slain conspirators came next: Catesby, Percy, the two Wrights, coupled with that of Francis Tresham, 'lately dead'. The names of the other three surviving conspirators, Robert Wintour, John Grant and Ambrose Rookwood, occurred in the course of the same indictment, an extremely long document which certainly did not underplay the drama of the occasion.

All seven of these conspirators pleaded 'Not Guilty', including Guy Fawkes. These pleas caused the authorities some surprise, as the previous confessions of the prisoners were 'notorious'. Guy Fawkes, in particular, had freely admitted his

---

* There was no mention of the statute under which they were being tried but it was presumably that of 1352 (25 Edw. st. 5 Cap. 2), which made it treason 'to compass or imagine the death of the king, his queen or the royal heir' (Bellamy, p. 9).

guilt from the first moment of his apprehension on 5 November. Digby had to be tried separately since, alone among his comrades, he pleaded 'Guilty'.

Sir Edward Phillips, Serjeant-at-Law, now sprang into action with what was termed the 'declaration'. His words were magisterial, eloquent and damning: 'The tongue of man never delivered, the ear of man never heard, the heart of man never conceived, or the malice of hellish or earthly devil ever practised...' such a treason. For if it was 'abominable to murder the least' of God's creatures, then how much more abominable to murder 'Such a King, Such a Queen, Such a Prince, Such a progeny, Such a State, Such a government...'.[25]

The Attorney-General Sir Edward Coke was the next to speak and he did not spare himself – or his audience. He made an extremely long speech, a fact he himself acknowledged when he used the word 'copious' of what was to follow: he did not intend to be 'so succinct as usual'.[26] One important aspect of this speech was however a negative one. Throughout, Coke implicitly denied that King James had made any promises of toleration to the Catholics before his accession. This was hardly surprising, given that Salisbury had written to Coke privately in advance in order to 'renew' his memory on the subject. Coke was to underline the fact that certain persons had gone to Spain to stir up an invasion 'as soon as the Queen's breath was out of her body'. This emphasis was the King's express wish and Salisbury explained his reason. The King was aware that there were some men who would suggest that only despair at the King's behaviour towards the Catholics, his severity, had produced 'such works of discontentment' as the recent treason.

The point was evidently important to James and one can guess why. Those vague Scottish promises of toleration were now a very long way away in the King's scope of things and such politically embarrassing intrigues of another time, another country, were best not recalled. It was far better to present the Catholics as a nest of malcontents from the word go, plotting to destroy the King 'before his Majesty's face was ever seen' – that is, in advance of his arrival in England. One may perhaps hear the delicate whisper of the King's guilty conscience in this firm rebuttal.

Salisbury's further instructions – all in his own handwriting – were interesting too. Monteagle was to be lauded for his part in the discovery of the Plot, but care was to be taken by Coke not to vary from the King's own account, already published. Coke, in short, was not to give credence to a story 'lewdly given out' that Monteagle had once been part of the Plot, and had betrayed it to Salisbury, still less that one of the conspirators had actually written the anonymous letter. (Monteagle's name was also obliterated in the published account of the Spanish Treason, as related by Francis Tresham.) Salisbury's last note was characteristic: 'You must remember to lay Owen as foul in this as you can.'[27]

Coke did not fail Salisbury and he did not fail King James. The Spanish Treason, including the two thousand horses promised by the English Catholics, featured strongly. So did the oaths taken by the conspirators and the alleged administration of the Sacrament – by Garnet, Tesimond and other Jesuits – to sanctify them. (Guy Fawkes' specific denial while being examined that Father Gerard knew anything of the Plot when he gave the Sacrament in May 1604 was not mentioned. To make quite sure this damaging statement was omitted, Coke underlined the passage in the examination in red and marked in the margin 'hucusque' – thus far and no further.)[28]

The Spanish King was however courteously handled. His Ambassador, listening intently in his private closet, must have been relieved to find that 'foreign princes' were (by the King's direct instructions) 'reverently and respectfully spoken of'. The priests, in contrast, were execrated. Their traitorous advice, their outright encouragement were underlined at every point, giving a picture of the Jesuits' behaviour which was so far at variance with the truth that it would have been laughable if it had not been so tragic – and so sinister.

With a flurry of classical and Biblical quotations, Coke

described the Powder Treason as having three roots, all
planted and watered by the Jesuits. 'I never yet knew a treason
without a Romish priest,' he declared, 'but in this, there are
very many Jesuits.' In short the 'seducing Jesuits' were the
principal offenders. All the old stories of the Jesuits seeking to
remove crowns from rulers were trotted out, how the practices
of 'this sect' principally consisted in 'two Ds, to wit, the deposing of kings, and disposing of kingdoms'. As for absolution,
Catesby had received it in advance from the Jesuits and been
encouraged to believe that his potential crime was 'both lawful
and meritorious'. After that, 'he persuaded and settled' the rest
of the Plotters when they raised some doubts, telling
Rookwood, for example, that Father Garnet had given him
absolution for the action, even if it involved 'the destruction of
many innocents'.

The emotive subject of equivocation was also introduced by
Coke. This was the art of lying as practised by Catholics – or
so the government would have it. (The Catholics themselves,
as we shall see in the next chapter, viewed it rather differently.)
Coke spoke of how the 'perfidious and perjurious equivocating'
of the conspirators, abetted and justified by the Jesuits, had
allowed them not only to conceal the truth but also to swear to
things which they themselves knew to be totally false. This was
because 'certain heretical, treasonable and damnable books',
including one which Coke entitled 'Of Equivocation', had been
discovered among Francis Tresham's possessions. It was a
subject to which Coke would return with eloquence in the
future. In the meantime, the shade of Francis Tresham was
beginning to haunt Father Garnet.

Coke's editorial concoction of what had actually taken place
was accompanied by an even more colourful evocation of the
horrors which might have taken place. Coke focused in turn on
the probable fate of the Queen, Prince Henry 'the future
hope', and, in a sense worst of all, the young Princess
Elizabeth – 'God knoweth what would have become of her.'
As he got into his stride, Coke even managed to feel sorry not
only for the men and beasts who would have suffered from

the explosion but also for the very buildings of the neighbourhood: 'insensible creatures, churches and houses, and all places near adjoining' – a remarkably modern concern.

When, however, Coke came to his delineation of the penalties traditionally meted out to traitors, he showed himself a man of his own time. Each condemned prisoner would be drawn along to his death, backwards at a horse's tail because he 'hath been retrograde to nature': his head should be near the ground, being not entitled to the common air. He was to be put to death halfway between heaven and earth as unworthy of both. His privy parts were to be cut off and burnt before his face since he himself had been 'unworthily begotten' and was in turn unfit 'to leave any generation after him'. The bowels and heart which had conceived of these terrible things were to be hacked out and the head 'which had imagined the mischief' was to be cut off. Thereafter the various dismembered portions of the traitor's body were to be publicly exposed, that they might become 'prey for the fowls of the air'.

When Coke's speech was concluded, the various 'Examinations, Confessions and voluntary Declarations' of the prisoners were read aloud.[29] These began with the testimonies by Guy Fawkes and Francis Tresham about the Spanish Treason, Tresham including the names of Father Garnet and Father Tesimond as being 'acquainted with Wintour's employment in Spain'. After this followed the specific confessions to do with the Powder Treason. Guy Fawkes' confession came first, followed by the confession of the recently captured Robert Wintour. This had been taken on 17 January in front of the Lords Commissioners, and was accompanied by a long statement signed by him four days later.

This statement had an important postscript: 'I confess that on Thursday 7th of November, I did confess myself to Father Hammond the priest, as other gentlemen did, and was absolved, and received the Sacrament.' Hammond was in fact the alias of the chaplain at Huddington, Father Hart. The general confession of the conspirators at Huddington in the small hours of the morning was probably more to do with their expectation of death in the near future than with their guilt over the past. Nevertheless, the notion that the conspirators had been able to make a clean breast of their potential crimes and receive absolution from a priest – a Jesuit – two days after the discovery of the Plot was a damaging one.

More confessions were read, including that of Thomas Wintour as well as the examinations of Rookwood and Keyes. The last piece of evidence was not a confession, but it concerned a conversation which Robert Wintour was said to have had with Guido in the Tower after his capture. The two men found themselves in adjacent cells and took the opportunity to have what they believed to be an intimate conversation but was in fact overheard by a government spy. Wintour and Guido mentioned the taking of Nicholas Owen – 'the little man'. Then Robert Wintour said something to Fawkes to the effect that 'God will raise up seed to Abraham out of the very stones', meaning that God in the future would raise up others for the good of the Church, 'although they [the conspirators] were gone'.[30] These confidences were less important than the revelation of the government's methods of espionage among their prisoners. Sadly, Father Garnet never got to hear of this particular trick, otherwise his own conduct in the Tower might have been different.

After this evidence was heard, the seven were allowed at last to speak if they so wished, 'wherefore judgement of death should not be pronounced against them'. Only Ambrose Rookwood elected to make any real use of this privilege.[31]

Rookwood admitted that his offences were so dreadful that he could not expect mercy, and yet maybe there were some extenuating circumstances since he had been 'neither author nor actor', but had been drawn into the Plot by his feelings for Catesby, 'whom he loved above any worldly man'. In the end Rookwood craved for mercy, so as not to leave 'a blemish and blot unto all ages' upon his name and blood. Kings, he hoped, might imitate God who sometimes administered bodily punishments to mortals, but did not actually kill them.

The rest of the conspirators spoke shortly. Tom Wintour,

clearly suffering from remorse at having brought Robert into the Plot, asked to be hanged on behalf of his brother as well as himself. Guy Fawkes gave an explanation for his plea of 'Not Guilty' which had earlier baffled the court. He had done so, he said, in respect of certain conferences mentioned in the indictment 'which he knew not of'. The reaction of Robert Keyes was terse and stoic: death was as good now as at any other time, he said, and for this cause rather than for another. Thomas Bates and Robert Wintour merely asked for mercy.

John Grant kept up his reputation for taciturnity by remaining completely silent for a while. He then said that he was guilty of 'a conspiracy intended but never effected'. In a memorable phrase in the course of his speech, Coke had said that 'Truth is the daughter of Time [*Veritas temporis filia*]; especially in this case.' But John Grant's economical comment made before Time had had a chance to give birth to Truth was probably as just a verdict as any. It was indeed a conspiracy intended – but never carried out.

The trial of Sir Everard Digby followed. He pleaded 'Guilty' swiftly to the indictment, in order to have the privilege of making a speech. It was evidently not unmoving to some of those that heard it. Digby gave as his first motive his friendship and love for Catesby – how enduring was the influence and charisma of Robin! The cause of religion for which he had decided to neglect 'his estate, his life, his name, his memory, his posterity, and worldly and earthly felicity' took second place.[3a]

He alluded to the broken promises of toleration – the King cannot have liked that – as well as mentioning the recusants' fear of harsher laws in the coming Parliament. This referred specifically to the subject of recusant wives, the fear that women as well as men would be liable for fines. Digby then argued passionately that since his offence was 'contained within himself' the guilt of it should not be passed on to his family, least of all to his little sons. His wife – the unfortunate, destitute Mary – should have her jointure, his sisters their marriage portions and his creditors their debts; his man of business should be admitted to him so that these arrangements could be made.

Coke, however, made short work of all this. The precious friendship with Catesby was 'mere folly and wicked conspiracy'; Digby's religion was 'error and heresy'. Over the question of the wives, Coke laid all the blame for their recusancy squarely on their husbands' shoulders in a fine seventeenth-century flourish. Either a man had married a woman knowing her to be a recusant, in which case he must expect to pay a fine, or she had become a recusant subsequent to her marriage, in which case the husband was equally at fault for not having kept her under better control. As for Digby's children! Coke sneered at Digby's pretended compassion for them when he had so easily accepted the prospect of the deaths of other people's children, including the 'tender princes'.[33]

Digby interrupted here – even now, he had enough spirit not to be cowed by Coke. He did not justify what he had done, Digby said, and he confessed that he deserved 'the vilest death'; he was merely a humble petitioner for mercy and 'some moderation of justice' for his family. By way of answer, Coke quoted back to Digby a singularly relentless passage from the Psalms: 'Let his wife be a widow, and his children vagabonds, let his posterity be destroyed, and in the next generation let his name be quite put out.'

Northampton was the next to make a speech, referring in elaborate terms to the favour which had been shown Digby by the late Queen Elizabeth and by King James. Northampton, too, was determined to put an end to the rumours that before he inherited the English crown King James had promised 'some further hope and comfort' for the Catholics. So he held forth on the subject of James' lifelong Protestantism: that faith which James 'had sucked from the breast of his nurse' (but not of course from the breast of his Catholic mother – for once, the name of Mary Queen of Scots was not dragged in). Lastly Salisbury himself thought it necessary to return to the theme of the King's alleged promises yet again. No promises had been broken. There were no promises. Never at any time had King James given 'the least hope, much less promise of toleration'.[34]

At the conclusion of Salisbury's speech, Serjeant-at-Law Phillips asked for the judgement of the court on the seven conspirators found guilty, and upon Sir Everard Digby, guilty on his own confession. After a few remarks from the Lord Chief Justice, the jury was directed to consider its verdict. It can have surprised no one present in Westminster Hall on that icy late January day that the verdict was equally chilling: Guilty, all of them.

The Lord Chief Justice then pronounced judgement of high treason upon all the prisoners. Seven of them listened to him in silence. Once more the exception was Sir Everard Digby. As the court rose, Digby cried out impulsively: 'If I may but hear any of your lordships say, you forgive me, I shall go more cheerfully to the gallows.' His speech had aroused a feeling of compassion if not of mercy – or perhaps it was his youth, the nobility of his bearing, the sense of utter waste. For the lords told him: 'God forgive you, and we do.'

PART FIVE

The Shadow of Death

He discovereth deep things out of darkness, and bringeth
out to light the shadow of death.

quoted in the Tower of London Memorial of the Powder Treason

CHAPTER FIFTEEN

The Heart of a Traitor

~⌒~

Behold the heart of a traitor!
Traditional cry of the executioner

The eight condemned men were put to death in two batches on consecutive days. On Thursday 30 January, Sir Everard Digby, Robert Wintour and John Grant were fetched from the Tower of London and Thomas Bates was brought from the Gatehouse. The time for executions was around eight o'clock in the morning, dark and bleak at this time of year. The site chosen on the first day was the western end of the churchyard of St Paul's 'over and against the Bishop of London's house'. Not everyone, however, approved of the decision. Sir Arthur Gorges, a poet and a friend of Ralegh, who had sailed with him against the Spaniards, protested to Salisbury against the quartering of 'these wicked and bloody conspirators' being carried out in a place of such 'happy memory', for it was here that Queen Elizabeth herself had thanked God for her nation's deliverance from the Armada.[1]

The custom of conveying certain miscreants to their place of death by dragging them at the horse's tail, to which the Attorney-General had alluded at the trial, tended to rob the executioner of the material upon which to do his appointed work. The damaging ordeal also robbed the public of the full ceremony, which it much enjoyed. This included speeches from the condemned men as well as those prolonged indignities to still-breathing bodies so graphically described by Sir Edward Coke. Therefore, in the case of important prisoners such as the Powder Plotters, it was government policy to convey them singly, each strapped to a wicker hurdle, used as a kind of sledge.[2]

This open passage through the crowd had, however, its own dangers. First, there was the possibility – however remote – of rescue. Secondly, in the case of known Catholics, tiresome recusant devotions might interrupt the desired spiritual process of last-minute repentance. Thirdly, there was the question of the wretches' wives and womenfolk, who had not seen their men for several months, since that dreadful day in early November when the reckless stand at Holbeach had been planned.* Recusants' wives, or the friends of condemned priests, often tried to say a last goodbye in this manner. Thus armed men were stationed at doorways along the route from seven in the morning: 'one able and sufficient person with a halberd in his hand' for every dwelling house in the open street.[3]

Even so, the women managed to get themselves into the crowds, and at the windows. There is a story of one little Digby boy calling out, 'Tata, Tata,' at the moment when his father was being drawn by on his hurdle, his face low down so that, in Coke's words, he should not pollute the common air. Thomas Bates' wife Martha was one of those who managed to find a place in the crowd; she was rewarded by finding that her husband was on the leading hurdle, presumably because he had joined the melancholy procession from the other direction, the Gatehouse being in Westminster. Eluding the halberdiers, Martha Bates managed to throw herself on her husband as he lay on his hurdle; she wailed aloud against the wretched fortune which had brought him to this 'untimely end'.

---

* There is a tradition that Robert Wintour's wife Gertrude had various secret meetings with her husband during the two months he was on the run; but, given the persistent official attention to Huddington as a known recusant centre, one wonders whether either of them would have run the risk – for the future of their children was at stake.

Bates, practical man to the last, took the opportunity to tell Martha where he had deposited a bag of money (originally entrusted to him by Jack Wright), and he begged his wife to hang on to it for her own relief and that of their children. Afterwards Martha got into trouble with the authorities over this bequest – perhaps they thought Bates' last instructions had been on some more conspiratorial level. But in the end she was allowed to keep the money.

At St Paul's, Sir Everard Digby was the first to mount the scaffold. He had spent his last days in the Tower writing letters to 'my dearest wife' Mary and then to Kenelm and John.[4] He urged the latter pair to support each other as brothers, and avoid the bad examples of Cain and Abel, and Philip of Macedon's sons (one of whom had murdered the other). Otherwise Everard Digby wrote poetry which expressed his own resignation to his fate – and explains perhaps further the affection in which contemporaries, even religious enemies, held him:

Who's that which knocks? Oh, stay, my Lord, I come:
I know that call, since first it made me know
Myself, which makes me now with joy to run
Lest he be gone that can my duty show.
   Jesu, my Lord, I know thee by the Cross
   Thou offer'st me, but not unto my loss.

In spite of Digby's resolution and his 'manly aspect', it was noted that his colour was pale and 'his eye heavy'. But he was determined to speak out strongly. He declared that he held what he had done to be no offence, according to his own conscience, informed by his own religion, but he acknowledged that he had broken the law. For this, he asked forgiveness of God, of the King and of the whole kingdom. Even at this moment, however, Digby took pains to deny that Father Gerard or the other Jesuits had known anything of the Plot. He then refused to pray with the attendant Protestant preachers and instead took refuge in 'vain and superstitious crossing', as one hostile observer noted, and 'mumbling to himself' in Latin.[5]

These private Catholic devotions performed, Digby reverted to the gallant courtier he had always been in public. He said goodbye to all the nobles who had been his friends – it was established procedure that dignitaries should witness state executions – with careful attention to their rank. He spoke to them all, as they said to each other afterwards, in such a cheerful and friendly manner, 'as he was wont to do when he went from Court or out of the City, to his own house in the country'.[6]

What followed however was not to be so casual or so pleasant. Digby was hung from the halter for a very short time before being cut down and he was therefore fully conscious when he was subjected to the prescribed penalties. Anthony à Wood had an extraordinary story to tell about what happened next.* 'When the executioner plucked out his heart and according to the manner held it up saying "Here is the heart of a traitor", Sir Everard made answer: "Thou liest".' Even if such a spirited riposte – any riposte – would have been anatomically possible under the circumstances, the fact that such a story was told is still further proof of the esteem in which Sir Everard Digby was held. As it was, the common people 'marvelled at his fortitude' and talked 'almost of nothing else'.[7]

Robert Wintour was the second to ascend the scaffold. He said little and was praying quietly to himself as he went to his death. John Grant, coming next, was the only one of the conspirators who actually justified what they had tried to do, and refused to confess to any offence, for it had been 'no sin against God'. A report by Salisbury to Edmondes in Brussels confirmed this obduracy. It was a defiance which was later embroidered by Protestant propaganda, with Grant claiming that the spiritual merits of the Plot would expiate all the sins he had committed in his life. 'Abominably blinded' by the fire

---

* He was writing long after the event but with information derived from Francis Bacon, who would have been present at the execution.

at Holbeach, he allowed himself to be led quietly up the ladder to the halter, resistance being impossible. After crossing himself, he went to his death.[8]

From the point of view of the onlookers, Thomas Bates was a more satisfactory criminal than these men with their crossings and their mumbled Latin prayers. If you could not be valiant – though misguided – like Sir Everard Digby, it was better to be abjectly penitent like Bates. He spoke of being inspired by affection for his master, Catesby, which had caused him to forget his duty 'to God, his King and Country'. This led Father Gerard to say afterwards that it was 'no marvel' that Bates had shown less courage than his companions, since he had acted for human rather than divine love; but Gerard concluded his verdict on a charitable note: 'It is to be hoped he found mercy at God's hands.' In general, Bates seemed deeply sorry for what he had done. He asked forgiveness of God and he also asked forgiveness of the King, and of the whole kingdom, praying humbly for 'the preservation of them all'.[9]

The four remaining executions took place in the Old Palace Yard at Westminster the next day, Friday 31 January. Possibly the patriotic reproaches of Sir Arthur Gorges had found echoes on other breasts, but more likely it was intended to put to death the major criminals – Tom Wintour and Guy Fawkes – in the very place which they had planned to demolish in order to hammer home the message of their wickedness. The route from the Tower was in consequence longer. In the course of it, Elizabeth Rookwood managed to watch her husband pass on his hurdle from the window of their lodgings in the Strand. As for Rookwood himself, he asked to be informed when he reached the appointed spot so that he could open his eyes and have one last glimpse of his beautiful wife (otherwise he kept his eyes shut in prayer). When he reached this point Ambrose Rookwood raised himself up as far as he could – he was tied with ropes – and called out: 'Pray for me, pray for me!'

'I will, and be of good courage,' his wife shouted back.

'Offer thyself wholly to God. I, for my part, do as freely restore thee to God as He gave thee unto me.'*[10]

Tom Wintour was the first of these men to mount the scaffold. He was 'a very pale and dead colour'. The spectators were anxious to hear a speech but Wintour, for all his pallor, riposted firmly that this was 'no time to discourse: he was come to die'. He too, like Digby, acquitted the Jesuits, including Father Tesimond, of all guilt, and asked for the prayers of all Catholics. Finally, crossing himself, he declared that he died a true Catholic. On the whole, professions of repentance were more likely to secure the hoped-for prolonged hanging which would result in unconsciousness. Although Tom Wintour had seemed 'after a sort, as it were, sorry for his offence', either his firm last-minute protestation of his Catholicism or his defence of the Jesuits denied him any relief. He was cut down after only 'a swing or two with a halter'.[11]

Ambrose Rookwood came next. He did choose to make a speech. This was a model of repentance, since he first freely confessed his sin in seeking to spill blood, and then asked God to bless the King, the Queen and all the 'royal progeny', that they might live long 'to reign in peace and happiness over this kingdom'. It was true that at the last Rookwood proceeded 'to spoil all the pottage with one filthy weed', in the words of an observer – evidently a Protestant – for Rookwood finally besought God to make the King a Catholic. But Rookwood's earlier sorrowful words seem to have been enough to secure him a long hanging, and he was more or less at his last gasp when he was cut down.[12]

Robert Keyes determined not to accept his fate passively. 'With small or no show of repentance', he went 'stoutly' up the ladder. Once at the top, and with his neck in the halter, he did not wait for the hangman's 'turn' but turned himself off, with a violent leap into space. His intention was presumably to die

---

* This is the version given by Father Gerard, who was not present; but it would have been pieced together carefully from the recollections of eye-witnesses: as was always done with the deaths of Catholics at the hands of the state, great trouble was taken to treasure the details of the final scenes.

quickly (although Father Gerard glossed this as meaning that Keyes wanted to die at a moment of his own choosing, with his mind set on his prayers, rather than be taken by surprise by the hangman). Unfortunately, the plan did not work. The halter broke, and he was taken, alive, to the quartering block.[13]

Guy Fawkes, 'the great devil of all', was the last to mount the scaffold. He did not make a long speech – he was probably not capable of it, since a contemporary reported his body as being visibly 'weak with torture and sickness'. He did ask forgiveness of the King and state, but at the same time kept up his 'crosses and idle ceremonies'. His last ordeal was to mount the ladder. He was scarcely able to do so, and had to be helped up by the hangman. Guido did, however, mount high enough for his neck to be broken with the fall.[14] Perhaps it was the physical punishment which he had endured in the months past which spared his consciousness at the end.

As Salisbury pointed out to Edmondes, all eight men had died Catholics. Nothing that had happened had caused them to abandon the religion for which they had sacrificed their liberty and finally their lives.

A few days after these executions, Father Garnet was sent for by the authorities to be brought to London. His treatment remained gracious, especially if one reflects on the recent ordeals of the men who were said to be his co-conspirators. While still at the house of Sir Henry Bromley, Father Garnet had been permitted to celebrate the lovely feast of Candlemas – the last feast of the Christian cycle before the beginning of Lent – together with Sir Henry and his family. A great white wax candle with 'Jesus' and 'Maria' on the sides, which had been confiscated at Hindlip, was produced. Father Garnet took it in his hands and passed it to Father Oldcorne, saying that he was glad to have carried 'a holy candle on Candlemas Day'. Then all present drank the King's health with their heads bared.[15] As an episode, it was a conspicuous illustration of the paradox of Catholic loyalty.

Nor was the Jesuit's dignity sacrificed in any way during the journey. Father Garnet was still very weak after his eight-day ordeal and his swollen legs were causing him pain. Salisbury ordered that he should be given the best horse, and his hospitality *en route* was paid for by the King (which meant that it was not stinted).

When a Puritan minister accompanying the cortège attempted to involve him in theological debate, Father Garnet immediately saw the dangers in this kind of exercise. Silence might be construed as inability to answer, while too impassioned a defence of the Catholic viewpoint could be held as evidence against him. Garnet consulted Sir Henry Bromley. The result was a discussion, in effect chaired by Sir Henry, in which the Puritan ranted at length without interruption, and Garnet then proceeded to speak 'briefly and clearly' as well as displaying remarkable erudition (the Puritans were wont to claim erudition as their special province). Sir Henry Bromley was much impressed and the egregious minister much disappointed.[16]

In London, Father Garnet was at first lodged in the Gatehouse prison in Westminster. His companion in hiding at Hindlip, Father Oldcorne, was also placed there, although housed in a separate cell. The arrival of the Superior of the Jesuits, with a fellow Jesuit, created a sensation in the Gatehouse prison. A flock of prisoners crowded at the entrance. Garnet cried out in a loud voice to know whether any of them were Catholics. When many replied that they were, Father Garnet responded: 'God help you all! And myself as well who come to keep you company here for the same cause.'[17] Father Garnet's nephew, Thomas Garnet, also a priest, who operated under an alias, was among the many Catholics currently held at the Gatehouse.

This interest in and response to Father Garnet draws attention to the ambivalent nature of Jacobean prisons as far as recusants were concerned. Prisons could serve as hotbeds of Catholicism, as well as centres for persecution. Paradoxically, it was often easier for recusants to attend a clandestine Mass in a prison containing priests than in the outside world. By modern standards, there was even a kind of informality prevalent in Jacobean prisons: inmates could send out to buy food, and, if necessary, could make purchases by stretching out money from prison windows. Obviously, more than mere food – information, letters – could be obtained by these means. In certain prisons, prostitutes and thieves would bribe their jailers to let them out under cover of darkness to go about their work, returning at dawn having earned the necessary money to make themselves comfortable.

Of the many prisons in the capital, one of them, the Clink, in Southwark near the present Blackfriars, was always full of Catholics: it has been described as a recusant 'propaganda cell for the whole capital'. Certainly Father Gerard had heard numerous confessions from his co-religionists when he was held there. Newgate, the chief criminal prison, also contained a 'great store of priests and other Catholics', to whom people of all sorts had 'continual access'.[18]

As for the Gatehouse, in January 1606 one of Salisbury's informants, Anne Lady Markham, complained about the sheer corruption of the place. Recusants were able to bribe their jailers to pass letters to their friends 'to tell what they have been examined of'; then they got back vital information which enabled them to guess 'shrewdly' how to answer.[19] Unfortunately the comparatively free conditions at the Gatehouse could also be used by the government for its own purposes. Unwittingly, Garnet's nephew, Father Thomas, was to be part of the entrapment which followed.

Another innocent agent was Anne Vaux, who with Thomas Habington's sister Dorothy (a convinced Protestant who had been converted into a fervent Catholic) had followed the Jesuits up to London, at a discreet distance. The two women lodged in Dorothy Habington's house in Fetter Lane, just off Fleet Street. They came into a London in which the main topic of discussion in official circles was religion and its consequences: this was emphasised by the House of Commons debate, a few days earlier, on the vexed subject of Protestant husbands having to pay the fines of their recusant wives. At the Plotters' trial, Sir Edward Coke had dealt with the matter tartly when Digby raised it, declaring that a recusant wife, one way or another, was always the husband's fault and he must pay up. But Sir Everard Digby's feelings were more in tune with the spirit of the times than those of the dismissive Coke. Members felt uneasy about the measure, and it was agreed that it should be 'further considered on'.[20]

The next day, 5 February, everyone felt much happier discussing the 'Armour and Munitions' to be seized from recusants, and their elimination from the army. Much virulent anti-Catholic talk followed. The Papists were divided into three, of which the first group, 'old, rooted, rotten', were unlikely to be reclaimed at this stage, but fortunately they were more superstitious than seditious. The second group, the converts (described as the 'Novelists'), were the greatest danger. As for the third, 'the future tense of the Papists' – its youth – this was a group which must be nipped in the bud, with great care taken that recusants should not get away with their own marriages and christenings, as opposed to those of the state. By the end of the month, the incoming Venetian Ambassador was struck by the universality of the discussion: 'here they attend to nothing else but great preparations for the annihilation of the Catholic religion'.[21]

This harsh talk from the male world did not mean that two recusant gentlewomen, both unmarried, could not manage to live at liberty in London. The social rule by which women were not persecuted to the hilt (as Martha Bates had been allowed her traitor husband's money for her relief) still obtained. So long as Anne Vaux remained quietly in Fetter Lane, living in the recusant world which was by definition discreet, she was unlikely to get into trouble. But of course for many years Anne Vaux had planned her life not so much to stay out of trouble as to help and protect Father Garnet. And that continued to be her motive in coming to London. She wanted news of him. She also wanted, if possible, to communicate with him directly.

Father Garnet's first examination in front of the Privy Council took place on 13 February.[22] His journey from the

Gatehouse prison to Whitehall did not pass unremarked. Father Garnet told Anne Vaux later that among other comments from the crowd he heard one man say derisively to another: 'There goes a young Pope.' The Council, however, treated him with outward respect. They addressed the Jesuit throughout as 'Mr Garnet' (they did not recognise his priesthood, but at the same time did not treat him with the contempt which would have been accorded a common criminal) and took off their hats when they spoke to him. These Councillors were the familiar band of Popham, Coke, Sir William Waad and Lords Worcester, Northampton and Nottingham, with Salisbury as their leader.

There was, however, one unpleasant indication of how the Council might promote derision in its own style. At some point in an early interview Salisbury leant forward and twitted the Jesuit about his relationship with 'Mistress Vaux' since Salisbury had intercepted a letter from her to the priest signed 'Your loving sister, A G'.

'What, are you married to Mrs Vaux! She calls herself Garnet. What, you old lecher [*senex fornicarius*]!' At the next interview, according to Garnet's account in a letter to Anne, Salisbury pretended to put the matter to rights. He put his arm around Garnet's shoulders and told him that he had spoken 'in jest'. The rest of the Councillors hastened to assure Garnet that they knew he led an exemplary life in that respect.[23]

If it was a jest, it was a strange one to make at that time and in that place to a middle-aged priest about his relationship with a Catholic spinster in her forties. But it was not a jest. On the contrary, it was part of a deliberate campaign to blacken the reputation of Father Garnet, so that the somewhat flimsy evidence which connected him to the Plot (of which he was supposed to be the leading conspirator) could be enhanced with hints of his personal depravity.

The charge was, inevitably, not an unfamiliar one in relation to celibate Catholic priests working clandestinely in England. Their very dependency on the women's domestic world, the false relationships to which they had to pretend for security's sake, meant that it was easy to spread such a smear. Father John Gerard had been charged with the same scandal concerning Lady Mary Percy, unmarried daughter of a previous Earl of Northumberland, who had founded the first English convent abroad since the Reformation. The accusation was made by Richard Topcliffe when Gerard was held in the Tower.

'It was you who stayed with the Earl of Northumberland's daughter,' said Topcliffe. 'No doubt you lay in bed together.' Even though Gerard knew Topcliffe was speaking 'without what even he considered the slightest evidence', the priest shook with anger at his indecency.[24]

Anne Vaux was not the only woman linked to Father Garnet (even though, according to the Councillors, his exemplary life was supposed to be well known). Dorothy Brooksby, from the prominent recusant family of Wiseman, was a young woman married to Anne Vaux's nephew William. Her two baby girls formed part of the extended household over which the Vaux sisters presided, and which included Father Garnet. At a later examination Coke taxed Garnet with attending a Catholic christening at White Webbs, and Sir William Waad went further, saying 'gibingly' that the priest was surely present at the baby's begetting also. Garnet protested against the unseemly insult as being not fit for 'this place of justice', at which Coke compounded it by suggesting that Mrs Brooksby's baby, being a priest's child, had 'a shaven crown'.[25]

This kind of crude badinage, however amusing for Coke and Waad, however distasteful to Father Garnet, was in a different class from the derogatory slant given to Garnet's twenty-year partnership – for that is the appropriate word to use – with Anne Vaux. For years, those who wished to denigrate the Jesuits had accused Garnet of effrontery – 'face' – in carrying a gentlewoman up and down the country with him.[26]

That partnership had indeed been at the very centre of recusant life. One of Digby's servants, examined about Father Garnet after his master's capture, unconsciously suggested a parallel between Anne and the Biblical Ruth: 'Mrs Anne Vaux doth usually go with him [Garnet] whithersoever he goeth.'[27]

Of course in one sense the relationship was paternal: Garnet was Anne Vaux's 'ghostly father', her spiritual director, and she was his penitent, his 'daughter in Christ'. Nevertheless it was a true partnership because without Anne Vaux's continuous, energetic, thoughtful loyalty Father Garnet could never have carried out his ministry in England for so many years without capture. But it was certainly not a partnership in any physical sense. Rather, it was a spiritual union, of the type experienced by saints in the Catholic Church such as St Francis and St Clare or the two founders of the Benedictine Order, St Benedict and another St Scholastica.

Unfortunately, as Father Gerard wrote later in this context: 'The sensual man perceiveth not these things which are of the spirit of God [*Animalis Homo non percepit ea quae Dei sunt*].' Garnet's enemies, in seizing on an apparent weakness, were measuring others by 'their own desires, not feeling any spark of that heat which moved so many Maries to follow Christ and his Apostles'. (Father Garnet himself, in bygone years, had sometimes in his thoughts likened Eleanor Brooksby and Anne Vaux, the widow and the virgin, to the two women 'who used to lodge our Lord'.)[28]

Of course no one who actually knew Anne Vaux credited the story. Her 'sober and modest behaviour' would impress even the government's interrogators. Anne Vaux was so manifestly that type of good woman, the backbone of many faiths, not only the Catholic one, who would 'willingly bestow her life' labouring to do God service.

She had never shown the slightest interest in getting married and her earliest struggles to obtain control of her fortune from Sir Thomas Tresham had been with the intention of using it to help the priesthood. Here was one who would surely have acted as a powerful abbess or reverend mother in pre-Reformation days. Many of Anne Vaux's similarly pious contemporaries had indeed fled the country to join the religious orders set up for expatriate Catholic women on the continent. Anne Vaux, encouraged by Father Garnet, discovered a different vocation: she was to be a practical and courageous Martha

in England, rather than a contemplative Mary in a convent in
Flanders.

Strangely enough, given the government's indictment of
Garnet at the head of the list of conspirators, his early examinations contained very few allegations about the Plot itself.
The smear concerning Anne Vaux might be unpleasant, but it
was not proof of treason. In general, Garnet's admissions to
the Council concerned those things of which he at least did
not feel ashamed: that he had been at Coughton on 1 November, and that he had received Catesby's explanatory letter of
6 November. But he steadfastly denied any complicity in the
Plot itself; nor did he reveal any names of conspirators.

What did take place at Garnet's interview while he was still
in the Gatehouse was a prolonged questioning on matters of
theology, including the doctrine of equivocation. Salisbury told
Garnet this was 'the high point' on which he had to satisfy the
King, in order to prove that he could be trusted as a loyal subject; in other words, that his was not the heart of a traitor. The
discussion was given a special emphasis by the fact that the
manuscript of a treatise on equivocation was lying displayed on
the Council Table.[29]

At this moment the Jesuit, convinced that the examination
was about details of the Powder Treason on which he could
clear himself, was unaware how much weight was going to be
attached to this subject. Nor indeed could he have foretold
how the malevolent image of an equivocating Jesuit, fostered
by Coke, would seize hold of the popular imagination.

The treatise had been among the 'heretical, treasonable and
damnable books' belonging to Francis Tresham to which Coke
had alluded at the trial of the Plotters. Coke had referred then
to the 'equivocating' – swearing to things they knew to be false
– by the conspirators: this, he said, had been encouraged and
justified by the Jesuits.[30] But Father Garnet of course had no
idea of the course of the trial: the only men who might have
warned him – the defendants – were already dead by the time
he reached London.

Since the book was to assume an enormous importance in the government's eyes, its discovery by Coke was either a lucky chance or a tribute to his sharp intelligence. It had happened like this: at the beginning of the previous December, Coke, who lodged in the Inner Temple, had the idea of searching a particular chamber there which Sir Thomas had obtained for the use of his two younger sons, Lewis and William, and where Sir Thomas himself sometimes stayed. Coke was rewarded. Two versions of the same book were found, one quarto and a folio copy of it in what turned out to be the handwriting of Francis' servant William Vavasour. What Coke did not realise, for some reason, was that Garnet had written the treatise himself. Coke imagined that he had merely made corrections. It was a strange oversight, given that the quarto was actually marked 'Newly overseen by the Authour and published for the defence of Innocency and for the Institution of Ignorants'.* But Garnet was asked only 'where and when he did peruse and correct' the treatise, and so was able – for what it was worth – to preserve his anonymity.[31]

The quarto version had originally been entitled *A Treatise of Equivocation*, but that title had in fact been crossed out, as Garnet pointed out to Salisbury. The title *A Treatise against Lying and Fraudulent Dissimulation* had been substituted (although the earlier title could still be made out). To Garnet, the alteration was an important one of clarification. Indeed, between the nature of Garnet's correction and the government's continued use of the original title lay the whole matter of the dispute between them. To Father Garnet, equivocation was a precise doctrine which had nothing to do with lying, a practice he roundly condemned. To the government, on the contrary, equivocation was not only lying but hypocrisy, since it wrapped a mantle of holiness round the lies.

What Coke had found, and now laid before the Councillors, had in fact been written by the Jesuit a few years earlier. The

---

* This quarto version is now in the Bodleian Library, with Garnet's corrections (and Coke's own marks) clearly visible (Bodleian, Laud MS., misc. 655). The folio copy in Vavasour's handwriting has disappeared.

inception of the treatise was due to a general disquiet on the subject of equivocation following the trial of Father Robert Southwell in 1595. This trial probably introduced knowledge of the doctrine into England, both among officials and among the public.

It is true that there were passages in the works of the Fathers of the Church which referred to the lawfulness of dissimulating under certain specific conditions. Furthermore, in late-sixteenth-century Europe numerous subjects, who differed from their rulers in religion, faced the problem of what has been described as 'secret adherence', which inevitably entailed a good deal of dissimulation along the way. It might well be impossible to profess one's true religion in public without vicious penalties or even massacre – this applied to crypto-Protestants in Catholic countries as much as to crypto-Catholics in Protestant countries. This kind of secret adherence was given the name Nicodemism by Calvin, after the Pharisee Nicodemus, a believer in Christ who out of fear visited Him only by night. It was a form of behaviour which received tacit acceptance.[32]

Equivocation as a particular method of procedure was, however, a novelty.* It was this procedure, rather than the mere fact of concealment, which seems to have caused general disquiet as a result of the Southwell trial. This disquiet, it must be emphasised, was shared by Catholics as well as by those Father Garnet called heretics; among the former, the 'strange' practice was 'much wondered at'.[33]

At Southwell's trial, Anne Bellamy, a Catholic woman who was the exception to the honourable record of her sex during this period, had testified that the priest had taught her to deny the truth in answer to the question 'Is there a priest in the house?' Francis Tresham's reaction was to have Vavasour make a copy of Garnet's treatise 'that we may see what they can say of this matter'. This was exactly the purpose for which Garnet had written the book.[34]

* The Oxford English Dictionary dates the use of the word in this doctrinal sense to 1599.

Equivocation was essentially a scrupulous way of behaving by Catholics who shrank from telling outright lies. 'He that sticketh not at lies, never needeth to equivocate': this observation by the Jesuit Robert Persons is at the heart of the doctrine of equivocation and central to its understanding. Father Garnet put it even more robustly: liars took 'a readier way to serve their turn, by plain untruths and evident perjuries'.[33] In times of danger, a flat lie to protect the truth (such as Thomas Habington's denial of the priests' presence at Hindlip) would be most people's instinct. In the same way, Catholic priests in front of the English authorities might have been expected to deny outright the truths which would have condemned them to death – notably the fact of their own priesthood. But they did not do so. Heroically, they attempted to balance the needs of their predicament with the prohibition of the Church on outright lying. Yet the lies they so painstakingly avoided, or believed they avoided, were of the nature that conspirators of all types – to say nothing of governments protecting national security – utter without a qualm.

The underlying principle of equivocation was that the speaker's words were capable of being taken in two ways, only one of which was true. A typical example, which caused a great deal of Protestant indignation, had occurred in February when a certain Father Ward swore to the Dean of Durham that he was 'no priest' – meaning, it transpired, that he was not 'Apollo's priest at Delphos'. Secondly, Father Ward swore that he had never been beyond the seas: 'it's true, sayeth he, for he was never beyond the Indian seas'. One can see the absurdity of this: at the same time one can admire the earnest conscience which found it necessary to justify such life-saving lies.

Obviously the authority of the questioner was an all-important point about equivocation, as well as the seriousness of the matter at issue. Father Robert Persons cited the case of a man who denied he was a priest to an unjust questioner, adding the mental reservation that he was not a priest 'so as I am bound to utter it to you'. As Father John Gerard wrote, the intention was not to deceive 'but simply to withhold the truth in cases where the questioned party was not bound to reveal it'.*³⁶ Furthermore, it could be argued that certain equivocating answers actually addressed themselves to the real question at issue. For example, the question ostensibly asked might be 'Are you a traitor?' A priest might therefore lawfully answer 'No' to his interrogator because, despite his priesthood, he knew himself not to be a traitor.

Father Garnet's treatise, because it was provoked by the trial of Southwell, took as its starting point the Bellamy question.³⁷ He justified the denial, saying that a Catholic could 'securely in conscience' answer 'No' when interrogated about the presence of a priest concealed in a house on the ground that he had a 'secret meaning reserved in his mind'. Similarly the question 'Did you hear Mass today?' could be answered negatively because the person interrogated 'did not hear it at St Paul's or such like'. Biblical precedents were meticulously cited in the cause of justifying equivocation, including the words of Jesus Christ himself. When Christ told his disciples that 'the girl is not dead but sleepeth', before raising Jaira's daughter from the dead, this was a form of equivocation. So was Christ's declaration that he did not know when the Day of Judgement was to be: since as God the Son he knew exactly when it was to be.†

Unfortunately there were severe disadvantages to the use of equivocation. A leading Catholic authority on the Gunpowder Plot has gone so far as to describe its use as 'the best weapon in Coke's armoury, and, admittedly, the Achilles heel of his opponents'. First of all, the practice gave an impression of insincerity, not to say deviousness, even to the recusants themselves. The Appellant priests, for example, enemies of the Jesuits, ridiculed the practice: 'in plain English', this was lying. This was something on which any government skilled in propaganda could easily build. Secondly, almost more damagingly,

* The real parallel was with a prisoner's plea of 'Not Guilty', as Father Gerard himself pointed out (Morris, *Gerard's Narrative*, p. ccxii).
† See Mark 13:32, where Christ observes: 'But of that day and that hour knoweth no man, no, not the angels which are in heaven, neither the Son, but the Father.' Matthew 24:36 is virtually identical.

the doctrine of equivocation could be presented as alien, somehow unEnglish, and thus used to underline the notion of the Jesuits as Roman spies with no allegiance to Britain. Anniversary sermons on 5 November would regularly denounce equivocation in strong language of unequivocal disgust.[38] At the trial, Coke, wondering aloud what the 'blessed' Protestant martyrs Cranmer and Ridley would have made of such 'shifts', argued that they would never have used them to save their lives.[39] Thirdly, the doctrine of equivocation could be belittled and mocked.

Father Garnet, in his treatise, was concerned to stress that the occasions when equivocation could be legitimately used were 'very limited'; anyone who swore upon his oath to a falsehood 'in cases wherein he was bound to deal plainly' committed a sin. But of course in the question as to which cases necessitated plain dealing by Catholic priests, and which did not, lay the crux of the dispute between Garnet and his captors. He might see himself as having a heart loyal to the King, but as a man imprisoned on a most serious charge he needed to convince the King's mighty Councillors. It was unlikely, however, that Salisbury, Coke and Popham wanted to be convinced.

On arrival in the Tower the next day, Father Garnet was housed comfortably enough. It took him time to get such items as bedding and coal for his fire, but he described his room as 'a very fine chamber'. He was allowed claret with his meals, as well as buying some sack out of his purse for himself and his neighbours.* Garnet even declared mildly that the dreaded Sir William Waad was a civil enough governor, except when Waad got on to the subject of religion, which caused him to indulge in 'violent and impotent [uncontrolled]' speeches.[40]

Father Garnet was lucky – for the time being at least. Others were not so lucky. On 19 February, the Privy Council

---

* No one ever drank water with their meals during this period – which would have been another kind of death sentence – so that it was a question of what kind of alcohol, beer being most common, was served. Private funds were also an essential component of even the most spartan regime in prison.

issued orders which allowed 'the inferior sort' of prisoners connected to the Powder Plot to be put to the torture.[41] The so-called inferiors included Little John and Ralph Ashley, as well as Father Strange, captured in the autumn, and the serving man from White Webbs, James Johnson. These orders, enlarged three days later, provided for those prisoners already in the Tower to be put to the manacles while other prisoners could be fetched thither for that purpose. The horrors were by no means over.

CHAPTER SIXTEEN

The Jesuits' Treason

❧

I will name it the Jesuits' treason, as belonging to
them...

SIR EDWARD COKE
March 1606

In the Tower of London, the torturing of the 'inferior' prisoners was pursued without pity. James Johnson was
believed to have been racked for four or five days, and on
one occasion, according to the official record, for three hours
at a time. His crime was to have worked for Father Garnet
under the name of 'Mr Meaze', at White Webbs. As a result of
torture, he identified Garnet as Meaze when confronted with
him. Ralph Ashley, suspected of having assisted Little John in
his work, was among the other servants who were tortured.
Father Garnet asked Anne Vaux to try to get hold of some
money belonging to the Society of Jesus, in order to provide
beds for the sufferers (the alternative for these broken bodies
was the floor of a dungeon and straw).[1]

Nor were the priests, including Father Oldcorne, spared.
Father Strange, that 'gentleman-like priest' who loved tennis
and music, was a victim because of his friendship with Catesby,
even though Strange had never been involved in the treason.
Like Johnson, who was released in August, Father Strange
lived out the rest of his life disabled, and 'totally incapable of
any employment', as a result of his sojourn in the Tower.[2]

Most brutal of all was the treatment given to Nicholas

Owen, better known to the recusants as Little John. Since he had a hernia caused by the strain of his work, as well as a crippled leg, he should not have been physically tormented in the first place: as Gerard wrote in his *Narrative*, 'the civil law doth forbid to torture any man that is broken'. But Little John, unlike many of those interrogated, did have valuable information about the hiding-places he had constructed: if he had talked, all too many priests would have been snared 'as partridges in a net'. In this good cause, the government was prepared to ignore the dictates of the law and the demands of common humanity. A leading Councillor, on hearing his name, was said to have exclaimed: 'Is he taken that knows all the secret places? I am very glad of that. We will have a trick for him.'[3]

The trick was the prolonged use of the manacles, an exquisitely horrible torture for one in Owen's ruptured state. He was originally held in the milder prison of the Marshalsea, where it was hoped that other priests would try to contact him, but Little John was 'too wise to give any advantage' and spent his time safely and silently at prayer. In the Tower, he was brought to make two confessions on 26 February and 1 March. In the first one, he denied more or less everything – knowing Oldcorne (or Hall), knowing Garnet, under that name or any of his aliases, let alone serving him. He even remained vague about his own aliases: it was reported that 'he knoweth not whether he is called Little John'.[4]

By the time of the second confession, long and ghastly sessions in the manacles produced some results (his physical condition may be judged by the fact that his stomach had to be bound together with an iron plate, and even that was not effective for very long). Little John admitted to attending Father Garnet at White Webbs and elsewhere, that he had been at Coughton during that All Saints visit, and other details of his service and their itinerary. However, all this was known already. Little John never gave up one single detail of the hiding-places he had spent his adult life constructing for the safety of his co-religionists.

The lay brother died early in the morning of 2 March. He died directly as a result of his ordeal and in horrible, lingering circumstances. By popular standards of the day, this was a stage of cruelty too far. The government acknowledged the fact in its own way by putting out a story that Owen had ripped himself open with a knife given to him to eat his meat – while his keeper was conveniently looking elsewhere – rather than face renewed bouts of torture. Yet Owen's keeper had told a relative who wanted Owen to make a list of his needs that his prisoner's hands were so useless that he could not even feed himself, let alone write.[5]

The story of the suicide was so improbable that neither Owen's enemies nor his friends, 'so well acquainted' with his character over so many years, believed it. Suicide was a mortal sin in the Catholic Church, inviting damnation, and it was unthinkable that a convinced Catholic like Nicholas Owen should have imperilled his immortal soul in this manner. This 'false slander' concerning his death was contrasted by Catholics afterwards with Little John's calm and steadfast demeanour in the Marshalsea, when he certainly knew what lay ahead but showed no fear. Father Gerard called Nicholas Owen's end a glorious martyrdom.* His jailer's words were different but equally evocative: he said, 'the man is dead: he died in our hands'.[6]

The emollient handling of Little John's master, Garnet, did not however cease immediately. With the exception of Sir William Waad's angry ravings on the subject of Catholicism – which in any case the priest tried to bear patiently – Garnet considered himself well treated. Even his personal jailer (his 'keeper') appeared to be full of kindness towards him. One can imagine the Jesuit's pleasure when this fellow, Carey, confessed that Garnet's patient conduct had made such an impression upon him that 'he had even conceived a leaning for the Catholic religion'.[7]

As a kindness – which had to be kept, naturally, an absolute

---

* The Catholic Church has recognised Nicholas Owen as a martyr; he was canonised in 1970.

secret – Carey volunteered to convey letters from Father Garnet out of the prison. Garnet took the opportunity to write to his nephew Thomas, the priest held in the Gatehouse. Then, as the ultimate favour, Carey placed Father Garnet in a cell in the Tower which had a special hole in it through which he could talk to the prisoner in the next cell. This was Father Hall – in other words the Jesuit Edward Oldcorne.

Perhaps Father Garnet should have been suspicious about such a helpful arrangement. He did not of course know of the government's similar behaviour concerning Robert Wintour and Guy Fawkes. Unlike Gerard and Little John, both veteran prisoners, Garnet had never done time in captivity, thanks in large part to the inspired activities of Anne Vaux. Father Garnet, far from being the wily manipulator of government depiction, was, as Father Tesimond would sum him up, 'a charitable man ... ready to believe all things, and to hope all things'.[8] He was not a worldly person, and as such did not fear the Greeks bearing gifts.

As a result, from 23 February, John Locherson and Edward Fawcett, two government observers, were able to overhear a series of conversations 'in a place which was made for this precise purpose'. (It was Locherson who had spied on Wintour and Fawkes.) The first conversation they reported introduced the name of Anne Vaux. Garnet had just heard that she was in London and was proposing to send her a note via Carey, who had offered to 'convey anything to her'. It was Anne Vaux, said Garnet, 'who will let us hear from all our friends'. There was an obvious risk for Anne in contacting her, but Anne – hopefully protected by the known 'weakness' of her sex – could play a vital role in passing on the recusant news. She could also supply Father Garnet with those necessaries which were essential to any kind of comfort in prison. Garnet proceeded to talk cheerfully to Oldcorne of his good relationship with Carey, how he had rewarded him financially already and proposed to go on doing so, quite apart from giving him 'a cup of sack' and another one for his wife. Garnet recommended Oldcorne to pursue the same course, including 'somewhat' for Mrs Carey.[9]

The task of the eavesdroppers was from time to time complicated by aspects of daily life in the Tower. For example, a cock crowed and a hen cackled at exactly the same time outside the window of the cell, drowning the priests' murmurs, and since the names of various peers such as Northampton and Rutland had been mentioned it was feared that vital confidences had been missed. Much of what the government's men overheard was innocent and touching, rather than damaging, although Father Garnet's admission to a human failing – that he had drunk too much wine on one occasion – would be held against him later. It emerged second or third hand in a letter by John Chamberlain, who had heard that the Jesuit was drinking sack in his confinement 'so liberally as if he meant to drown sorrow'. The two priests also took the opportunity to confess to each other (as they had last done at Hindlip).[10]

But there were promising passages in the spies' report. Garnet was concerned to inform Oldcorne about the content of his examinations in front of the Council for the latter's sake (what had and had not been admitted). He told his colleague that he expected to be interrogated further about certain prayers he had said at the time of the meeting of the last Parliament 'for the good success of that business'. Garnet added to Oldcorne: *'which is indeed true'*. The underlining of the last phrase in the report was done by Coke, who obviously intended to make out that Garnet had prayed for the success of the Powder Treason. What Garnet had actually prayed for was Catholic relief from persecution, but the phrase was all too easily twisted.[11]

Not only were Garnet's intimate conversations being monitored, but his clandestine correspondence with his nephew Thomas in the Gatehouse and with Anne Vaux was being similarly vetted. It was simple for Carey to take to the governor the letters he had promised to 'convey'. Some of these were copied and then taken onwards; some may have been altered; some letters may even have been forged altogether. Even those places where Father Garnet used orange juice to write the most secret passages were not safe. Waad was able to heat up the letter and read the contents, having either been forewarned by Carey, or else, as would be maintained later, made suspicious by the excessive size of the paper employed – a lot of it apparently blank – and the insignificant contents of the letters. However, words written in orange juice remain visible once they have been exposed to heat (as opposed to lemon juice, which becomes invisible once more when it is cold). These were some of the letters which were probably held back altogether.*[12]

Father Garnet's correspondence was shaped round a number of domestic articles essential for the daily round of a middle-aged prisoner. To Thomas Garnet, the Jesuit sent his spectacles wrapped in a long piece of paper which was apparently blank. He accompanied them with a note asking for the spectacles to be set in leather – 'and let the fold be fit for your nose' – and provided with a leather case. It was Anne Vaux who duly returned the spectacles to him. Her covering letter contained the optimistic phrase: 'If this come safe to you, I will write and so will more friends who would be glad to have direction.' She asked for spiritual guidance for herself – Garnet had been her protégé, but also her confessor for over twenty years and she needed a replacement (it is clear from their letters that neither the priest nor the woman was under any illusions about what the inevitable end of his imprisonment would be). She concluded, not with a signature – too dangerous – but with the simple words: 'O that I might see you.'[13]

That, decided the authorities who read the letter, was easily arranged. In the meantime, Father Garnet replied with a series of letters, between 26 February and 1 March, to 'his loving sister Alice'. In ink he acknowledged her presents of bedding and handkerchiefs, and asked for socks, a black nightcap and a Bible. In orange juice he warned her against the capture of more priests which might compromise the existing prisoners as well as themselves. 'Take heed no more of our friends come in to danger. It will breed new examinations.' He gave her practical

* Letters from Father Garnet to Anne Vaux which include passages originally written in orange juice are still in the Public Record Office; they can, therefore, never have reached their intended destination in this form (S.P. 14/216).

instructions for the reordering of the Jesuit organisation in England: Father Anthony Hoskins was to be the temporary Superior until a new one was chosen by the proper procedure.

As to Anne's obligation to him as her Father Confessor, he released her from it. Garnet implied that he would understand if she now decided to leave for Flanders and the placidly devout life of a convent there, a tranquillity which Anne Vaux had certainly earned. Yet if she could manage to stay in England, while somehow still getting to Mass and Communion, 'I think it absolutely the best.' In this case, Anne, her sister Eleanor Brooksby, her nephew William (and presumably the young mother Dorothy Brooksby) should lie low for a while.

At the end of February Father Garnet told Anne Vaux that the Council could find nothing against him 'but presumptions'. Such presumptions were not enough for a state trial since Parliament itself called for proper proof. Something better, something meatier would have to be established. The likelihood is that Father Garnet himself was put to the torture five days after the death of Little John on 7 March. As a result he made a 'Declaration' or confession the next day.[14]

It is true that torture can take many forms, and it is not absolutely clear which form was used on Father Garnet, only that, in the words of Father Tesimond, 'one suspects bad treatment somewhere'. Tesimond (who was by this time on the continent) believed that Garnet had been drugged, which would have been easy to achieve, given the draughts of sack he was imbibing, and which may explain the ease with which he was able to supply himself with wine. Then there was the question of sleep deprivation, an ageless technique of oppression which leaves no physical mark: Garnet was said to be confused, 'heavy with sleep, so that he could scarcely hold up his head or keep his eyes open' in front of the Commissioners. By early April, Garnet's 'partisans' in Brussels were spreading the news that he had confessed only after 'torments', including starvation and lack of sleep. This caused great annoyance to the English Ambassador there.[15]

It is possible the rack or manacles were merely shown to Father Garnet, and that imagination – the dread which had hung over him for so long – did the rest. The view does not however explain several references to a *second* proposed bout of torture which presuppose that a first one had already taken place. On 24 March Garnet himself protested that it was 'against common law' to torture someone over and over again for the same information, but the Councillors replied, 'No, not in cases of treason,' since that depended on the royal prerogative. In a letter to Anne Vaux of 11 April Garnet lamented the possibility of being tortured 'for the second time'. He resolved to tell the whole truth rather than face such an ordeal, accepting that he would die 'not as a victorious martyr' (as had Little John) but as a penitent thief. Another letter to Father Tesimond also talked of 'a second time'.[16]

No great attention need be paid to the fact that Father Garnet at his trial agreed with Salisbury that he had been well treated. The dialogue (for which of course we depend on the official record, not on any Catholic version) went as follows: Had not Garnet been well treated since his arrest? 'You have been as well attended for health or otherwise as a nurse-child' (infant at the breast). Garnet then replied: 'It is most true, my Lord, I confess it.'[17] Modern experience of show trials teaches us what to make of these public statements.

Torture of some sort did, however, make Father Garnet break at long last the seal of the confessional, which he had preserved with such agonies of conscience. His Declaration of 8 March was extremely dramatic.[18] By whatever method produced, it gave the government clear proof that, according to the law of England, Garnet had been guilty of misprision of treason – that is, of knowing about a treason in advance and not declaring it. And it was true, for in June 1605 Garnet had been told about Catesby's proposed conspiracy by Father Tesimond. Although Father Garnet had taken many steps to avert what he considered to be a catastrophe, he had not actually told the King or the English Council.

In order to clear himself of the graver charge of actual

treason – that he had personally directed the Powder Plot – Garnet decided to tell his interrogators 'the little that he knew'. Contrary to his previous denials, Garnet had known something of the plot beforehand, but he had heard it in such a way that, 'up to that moment, it could never have been lawful for him, without most grave offence to God, to breathe a word to a living soul'. This was because the seal of the confessional was 'inviolable'.[19] There was a direct conflict here between the common law of England – to which Mr Henry Garnet, born in Lancashire, was subject – and the doctrine of the Catholic Church – to which Father Henry Garnet, priest of the Society of Jesus, was bound. It was a conflict of loyalties which had been in theory possible ever since Father Tesimond came to him and made that walking confession.

When one of the Councillors asked the obvious question: why could he reveal the conversation now, in order to save his own life, and not do so earlier, 'in order to save the life of the King and peers of the realm', Father Garnet gave the orthodox Catholic reply. Breaking the seal depended on the will of the penitent (Catesby in this case), not that of the confessor. Catesby had decreed that, in the event of the Plot's discovery, the matter of his confession was no longer to be regarded as sacred. If ever Garnet should be 'called in question for being accessory unto such a horrible action', either by the Pope, by his Superiors or by the English state, he would 'have liberty to utter all that passed in this conference'. But there was no doubt that the image of the equivocating – deceitful, malevolent and ultimately self preserving – Jesuit was only deepened further by this revelation. As Salisbury observed on 9 March, it was 'a small matter' whether Garnet himself lived or died. The important thing was to demonstrate the treasonable practices of the Catholics and 'to prove to all the world' that it was for this reason, not for their religious beliefs, that they should be 'exterminated'.[20]

Some of the details of the Declaration may have been dictated or suggested by the government, notably the reference to Hugh Owen.[21] Garnet stated that Guy Fawkes told him he 'went over for Easter [to the continent] to acquaint Owen', adding, rather naively – or perhaps confusedly, given his state – 'which I never imagined before, nor thought any resolution to be in Fawkes'. But in general Garnet, while admitting to the fatal walking confession of Father Tesimond, stuck firmly to his thesis: his horror at the conspiracy, his sleepless nights after the confession, and his intense desire to get the Pope to forbid all such violent enterprises.

When the King was shown this confession in writing, he considered it 'too dry' and asked for something slightly more emotive. In particular, he wanted details of the nobles who were involved. But Garnet failed him on this subject yet again in his second Declaration.[22] Catesby, he said, had been close to the Earl of Rutland, yet did not try to spare him from the explosion. Even if Catesby had had some idea of disabling the (Catholic) Earl of Arundel to keep him from Parliament, he had avoided the company of Lady Derby and Lady Strange 'though he loved them above all others because it pitied him to think that they must also die'.

While Salisbury reported triumphantly in letters abroad that Garnet had declared the Powder Treason to be absolutely 'justifiable', this was at the very least a governmental equivocation. Garnet had justified his behaviour following the Catesby/Tesimond confession: but he had never justified the conspiracy itself.

Some time before 11 March, Anne Vaux was taken into custody. She managed to disentangle herself from the trap laid by the government only to fall a victim to something she could not combat – sheer force. The keeper, Carey, using his mother as a go-between, had in his usual helpful fashion appointed a rendezvous at the Tower so that Anne might catch sight of Father Garnet, if not actually speak to him. But on her arrival Anne found the whole situation extremely suspicious. There were 'such signs and causes of distrust' that she cut short her visit, not even attempting to glimpse the Jesuit. Then, with that characteristic prudence which had enabled her to protect priests for so many years, she did not return to her own lodgings, realising full well she would be followed. She went instead to Newgate prison, ostensibly to visit the Catholic prisoners there 'unto which many of all sorts had continual access'.[23]

The stratagem infuriated the authorities, who had expected to be led towards a nest of recusants. Anne Vaux was arrested and 'with some rough usage' carried back to the Tower as a prisoner. This was highly unusual, as women were hardly ever committed to the Tower, and Anne Vaux, an unmarried gentlewoman, was not even suspected of being an active Plotter. In the Tower she was interrogated on two occasions, 11 and 24 March.[24] Since Father Garnet was also undergoing further interrogations at the same time – including interviews with the King, who was delighted to discuss such theological (and treasonable) matters as the seal of the confessional – the intention was obviously to play one prisoner off against the other.

From Anne Vaux the government learnt of the existence of a recusant safe house at Erith in Kent, unknown to them before. Here her first cousin, Francis Tresham, had come between Easter and Whitsuntide in 1605 and talked to Father Garnet. Anne also confirmed various movements of the conspirators, including a visit of Catesby, Tresham and Tom Wintour to White Webbs when Father Garnet was present. She talked of going to St Winifred's Well with Lady Digby and others she would not name: 'she will not say that Whalley [Garnet] was there'. She mentioned the gathering for the Feast of All Saints at Coughton, although she protested she knew nothing of Father Garnet's allegedly inflammatory prayer on the text: 'Take away the perfidious people from the territory of the Faithful.' She remembered the visit to Rushton shortly after the death of Sir Thomas when Lady Tresham had kept to her mourning chamber, although Francis Tresham had entertained them at dinner.

Unfortunately, all these movements described by Anne Vaux placed Father Garnet firmly in touch with Francis Tresham in recent years. This was nothing but the truth, but it suited Coke's plans. The government had been put out by Francis Tresham's inconvenient deathbed recantation on the subject of

Garnet and the Spanish Treason. Coke, with his agile and unscrupulous mind, intended to twist this truth into yet another denunciation of the evil doctrine of equivocation.

The government, however, had no intention of taking seriously Anne Vaux's positive evidence about Garnet's horror at the Powder Treason. They took what they wanted from her statements and ignored the rest. Yet Anne Vaux appended in her own hand a pathetic postscript to her first examination: she was sorry to hear 'that Father Garnet should be any least privy to this wicked action, as he himself ever called it', because he had made so many protestations to the contrary ever since. At her second examination, the Council was anxious that Anne should confirm that Garnet, while at White Webbs, had incited Francis Tresham to rebellion. Instead of this, Anne Vaux recalled the priest perpetually exhorting his friend to patience: 'She remembereth that he used these words, "Good gentlemen, be quiet. God will do all for the best."' As to toleration, Garnet had declared: 'we must get it by prayer at God's hands, in whose hands are the hearts of princes.'

Anne Vaux's dignity and decency impressed the Councillors, although this would not inhibit Coke from introducing her name gratuitously into his prosecution speech at Garnet's trial. In any case, by this time, the lewdly enjoyable story of their association had spread far outside the confines of the Council Chamber.

The trial of Mr Henry Garnet – as the government called him – took place on Friday 28 March at the Guildhall. It was, said Coke, the last act of that 'heavy and doleful tragedy' commonly called the Powder Treason. Before the tribulations of the Tower, Garnet had been much weakened by that ordeal at Hindlip and his physical condition was now very bad. It was unlikely that he could walk the distance to the Guildhall. This posed a problem which Sir William Waad solved by delivering the Jesuit in a closed coach. There were those who interpreted this unusual measure as fear of the Catholics among the crowds – it had not been granted, for example, to the conspirators, many of whom were 'of better birth and blood' than Garnet. But it seems clear from Waad's correspondence that it was Garnet's weakness which provoked the change: he was, in Waad's words, 'no good footman'.[25]

The trial started at about nine-thirty in the morning and lasted, as in January, all day.[26] The King was once again there 'privately', as were many courtiers, both male and female, including Lady Arbella Stuart and Catherine Countess of Suffolk. But there is no mention of Queen Anne (who had attended the Plotters' trial) being present. Either tact, given her known Catholic sympathies, kept her away or else the Queen's pregnancy – her eighth child was due in June – made the occasion unsuitable.

Father Garnet, throughout the trial, stood in something 'like unto a pulpit' which enabled the curious to feast their eyes on this creature of irredeemable evil who had planned to kill them all, but who appeared before them now in the guise of an unassuming middle-aged man with thinning hair who needed spectacles.

The indictment began by citing Garnet's various aliases: 'otherwise Whalley, otherwise Darcy, otherwise Roberts, otherwise Farmer, otherwise Philips'. This was a ploy which enabled Coke to make play with the fact that 'a true man' would never have had so many appellations. Garnet was described as 'Clerk, of the profession of Jesuits'. The date chosen for his treason was 9 June 1605, when he was said to have conspired with the late Robert Catesby not only to kill the King and his son, but also to 'alter and subvert the government of the kingdom and the true worship of God established in England'. After that, Garnet was accused of conspiring with Tesimond, and Thomas Wintour and other 'false traitors' including Catesby, to blow up and utterly destroy King, Prince Henry, Lords and Commons with gunpowder.

Garnet pleaded 'Not Guilty' and he was also allowed to object to a juror, John Burrell, a merchant like the other members of the jury. No reason had to be given for the challenge,* but presumably Burrell was a specially venomous anti-Catholic. After that, there was a brief – comparatively speaking – address from the Serjeant-at-Law. Then Sir Edward Coke got under way. From first to last, he was concerned to make it clear that the recent conspiracy had been dominated by the priests: 'I will name it the Jesuits' treason, as belonging to them...' He indulged in a long historic survey of conspiracies in the previous reign, as well as the present one, in all of which, said Coke, the Jesuits, with their doctrines of 'King-killing' and 'Queen-killing', had been central. As for Garnet, he had had 'his finger' in every treason since 1586.

Coke spoke eloquently in order to cover up one tricky area in the prosecution case: the fact that Garnet had not actually been personally involved in the actions which had brought the other Plotters to their doom in the midlands. By English law, he was undoubtedly guilty of misprision of treason, as has been noted, since he himself had admitted to foreknowledge of the conspiracy; but the greater charge of treason needed a little more manipulation if it was to stick. Coke's solution was to declare that Garnet as the 'author' of the Plot was immeasurably more sinful than the conspirators who were the 'actors' in it (*Plus peccat author quam actor*). Coke enlisted the Book of Genesis to his aid. Here the serpent received three punishments 'as the original plotter', Eve two 'being as the mediate procurer' and Adam only one, 'as the party seduced'. Garnet was the serpent.

Having laid down these principles, Coke proceeded to flesh them out by outlining at length the course of the Powder Treason. He was concerned to leave out no recent conspiracy which could conceivably be used to cast odium on what had happened. Thus the Main and Bye Plots of 1603 were said to be joined with the Gunpowder Plot, like foxes joined at the tails, 'however severed in their heads'.

At every stage, Garnet was said to be involved, whether in

* Sir Edward Coke in his *Third Part of the Institutes of the Laws of England, concerning High Treason* ... merely wrote that Garnet challenged Burrell 'peremptorily, and it was allowed unto him by the resolution of all the judges' (p. 27).

March 1603, cheering on Catesby with a 'warrant' for his enterprise, or in the summer of 1605 when he was accused of sending Sir Edmund Baynham to Rome to get the Pope's approval of the treason (the exact reversal of the truth). Then in late November at Coughton he had openly prayed 'for the success of the great action', and according to Coke prayer was much more than mere consent. Lastly, Coke denounced Garnet himself in terms which had become extended since his speech at the previous trial: where once he had referred to the 'two Ds' of the Jesuit sect, he now called Garnet 'a doctor of five Ds, namely, of dissimulation, of deposing of princes, of disposing of kingdoms, of daunting and deterring of subjects, and of destruction'.

Coke now concentrated at some length on 'dissimulation' as represented by that Treatise of Equivocation, 'seen and allowed [actually written] by Garnet'. Equivocation, said Coke, was an offence against chastity, since the tongue (speech) and heart (meaning) should rightly be joined together in marriage; equivocating statements were 'bastard children', conceived in adultery. This elaborate image gave Coke the opportunity to refer to Garnet's own vows of chastity, which he had broken: 'Witness Mrs Vaux for his chastity.'

Equivocation was certainly one of the two main prongs of the government's attack. It was, however, when Coke came to the subject of Francis Tresham and his dying letter that he was able to denounce equivocation in the most effective terms. He asked permission to read the fatal letter aloud. This was the document which Tresham had 'weakly and dyingly subscribed'. In the course of it Tresham exonerated Garnet from the Spanish Treason, mentioning, according to Coke, that he had not seen Garnet 'for fifteen or sixteen years before'. This gave Coke an open opportunity to elaborate on the contradictory testimony of Garnet personally, as well as that of Anne Vaux, who was 'otherwise a very obstinate woman'. Both had given evidence of ample meetings 'within two years space' and also many times before. According to Coke, Tresham had taken to heart the lessons of the 'book of equivocation', which had been found in his lodgings, and given vent to 'manifest falsehoods' even as he lay dying.

Garnet, never having seen Tresham's letter – despite the latter's instructions that he should do so – was in no position to contradict Coke's magisterial statements. But, for all Coke's indignation about a man who would equivocate on his deathbed, poor Tresham had not actually done so. His letter in fact referred to the long gap before 1602, not 1605.[27] All Garnet could do, however, was mutter lamely: 'It may be, my Lord, that he meant to equivocate.' It was just the kind of damaging admission that Coke wanted.

At various points in the trial, a great deal of time was spent in reading aloud statements. The first batch concerned plots encouraged by the Jesuits to assassinate Queen Elizabeth; then came extracts from the confessions of the conspirators – including Francis Tresham's original confession of 13 November in which he had implicated Garnet in the Spanish Treason and mentioned Monteagle. But times had changed: Monteagle was now an official hero for his association with the letter. Consequently, his name was omitted in court (the erasure can still be seen in the official document). Lastly, extracts from Garnet's own confessions were read aloud as well as those of Anne Vaux, and an account of his conversations with Oldcorne.

The Jesuit was however allowed to speak himself. He did as well as he could under the circumstances, although he could scarcely hope to extinguish the leaping flames of hatred – especially on the subject of equivocation – which Coke had ignited. His arguments in defence of the doctrine were those of his treatise. They included the words of Christ on the Last Judgement Day: 'in his godhead' Christ knew well when the day of judgement should be, but he did not know it 'so as to tell it to men'. Garnet explained that he had denied his conversation with Oldcorne because it had been a secret. In matters of Faith, however, Garnet stated firmly that equivocation could never be lawful.

The power of the Pope to excommunicate the sovereign of

a country, thus releasing his (or her) subjects from obedience, was the area of Garnet's weakness, as it had always been for Catholics because of the possible conflict of loyalties. Garnet argued valiantly enough, pointing to the fact that James had never been excommunicated. When he found the King 'fully settled' into his English kingdom, Garnet had burnt the briefs from the Pope calling for a Catholic successor to Elizabeth, and had constantly denied that these briefs legitimised any violent enterprise. Salisbury however pursued the point: if the King were to be excommunicated, were his Catholic subjects still bound to continue in their obedience? Garnet 'denied to answer', the most prudent thing he could do.

Coke now dismissed all Garnet's protests that he had tried hard to dissuade Catesby, and denounced equivocation yet again as 'open and broad lying and forswearing'. He also made little of the so-called seal of the confessional. The dismissal of this pretext – as the government considered it – was the other main theme of the trial. Under canon law, said Coke, Garnet could perfectly well have disclosed the matter communicated to him by Tesimond since it was 'a future thing to be done, not then already executed'. Others joined in the fray. The Earl of Northampton, who had a reputation as a public speaker, vented his talent to the full in a series of sonorous phrases. From Garnet's point of view, the most unfair of these was the Latin tag, *quod non prohibet cum potest, jubet*: what a man does not forbid when he can, he orders. Garnet asserted yet again that he *had* forbidden the treason.

But then this, like the earlier trial of the conspirators, was a showpiece. The odds had been weighted against Garnet from the beginning. Although treason as such – the charge on the indictment – was certainly never proved against him, misprision of treason was another matter. It was after all not likely that an English court would recognise the heavy burden that the seal of the confessional placed upon a Catholic priest (it was not part of common law).*

* Under English law today, Father Garnet would still be obliged to disclose the information he had received in the confessional from Father Tesimond, relevant

The matter was not dismissed without debate. Salisbury, by a characteristic sleight of hand, denied that there was such a thing as the seal of the confessional, and proceeded to demonstrate that Tesimond's observations had not been made under these privileged circumstances anyway. The ingenious mind of the great man, grappling with the net in which he intended to trap his adversary, can be traced in Salisbury's own handwritten comments on the subject in the state papers.[28] Examining Garnet, he pointed to the three necessary component parts of a Catholic confession. 'Satisfaction' had to follow contrition and confession, and without full repentance there could be no satisfaction. Since Catesby had not promised Tesimond to hold back from 'this evil act' he had not made a full repentance; the original confession was invalid, and Tesimond (and later Garnet) released from the seal.

Salisbury then made the quite different point that Garnet could have disclosed the conspiracy out of his 'general knowledge' of Catesby, following that conversation about the death of the innocents which was not privileged. Garnet's only answer to this was that he had not understood the significance of the conversation at the time. All along the King himself with his theological bent showed a keen interest in this topic. He had taken the opportunity to interview Garnet personally on the subject before the trial, and it was probably James who framed the questions subsequently put to him in court.[29] The key question was 'whether a priest is bound to reveal a treason dangerous to King and State if discovered unto him in confession, the party signifying his resolution to persist'. To this Garnet's answer was: 'The party cannot be absolved unless he come to submit himself; but the confessor is bound to find all lawful means to hinder and discover the treason.' This of course Garnet strongly

to Catesby's conspiracy. Under Section 18 of the Prevention of Terrorism (Temporary Provisions) Act 1989, it is an offence, punishable by up to five years' imprisonment, not to disclose information concerning an intended terrorist action. This applies to priests (as well as, for that matter, doctors and psychiatrists). Only lawyers can claim privilege in not revealing information received from their clients. (*Halsbury's Statutes of England and Wales*, 4th edn, 1994 reissue, 12, pp. 1339–40.)

maintained he had done. But the truth was that in the crucible of the Gunpowder Plot the responsibilities of a subject and of a priest were irreconcilable.

After all the sound and fury, the jury of wealthy London citizens took only fifteen minutes to deliver their verdict. Mr Henry Garnet, chief of the Jesuits, was found guilty of treason for conspiring to bring about the destruction of the King and government by the Powder Treason. The prisoner was asked, according to the law, whether there was any reason why judgement should not be passed. Garnet merely referred himself to the mercy of the King and God Almighty. The judgement, duly pronounced, was that he was to be hanged, drawn and quartered.

It had been a foul, wet spring while Father Garnet and his fellow prisoners languished in the Tower of London. The day after his trial, a westerly gale of hurricane intensity swept over England and on across the North Sea, destroying churches in the Low Countries. There had been nothing like it since 1570 – the year of the Pope's Bull excommunicating Queen Elizabeth, which had done so much to imperil the Jesuits in England.[30]

Dudley Carleton told John Chamberlain that Garnet had the air of being greatly surprised when finally told he was going to die: 'he shifts, falters and equivocates'. But, Carleton added gleefully, he will be 'hanged without equivocation'.[31] There is no other evidence of Garnet's faltering from what was surely an inevitable fate given the verdict of the trial. Carleton's comment merely symbolises the absolute obsession with the subject of equivocation in the minds of the public which followed upon the trial of Henry Garnet.

It did in fact take some weeks for Garnet to be hanged, with or without equivocation. Father Oldcorne, John Wintour, Humphrey Littleton and Ralph Ashley were put to death in the usual manner at Redhill, near Worcester, on 7 April, Father Oldcorne calling upon the name of St Winifred at the last. John Wintour, luckier than his two step-brothers, whose bodies were put up for public display, was allowed to be buried back at Huddington. There his body still lies in the Chancel 'under playne stones', along with that of his widowed sister-in-law Gertrude. Perhaps in the end the government heeded his plea that he had joined the conspirators at Dunchurch out of 'ignorance and not malice'. Humphrey Littleton met his death saying that it was deserved 'for his treason to God' in betraying the whereabouts of the two priests. Stephen Littleton and Henry Morgan were executed at Stafford.[32]

It was, however, the middle of Lent, Easter being very late in 1606 (Easter Sunday was not until 20 April, almost at the end of the possible cycle). This was not thought a suitable season for the great public festivity which the execution of the chief Jesuit would constitute in London. But the day eventually chosen – 1 May – seemed likely, on further consideration, to produce altogether too much festivity, not necessarily of the desired sort. Father Garnet reacted angrily to the unseemly news. 'What, will they make a May game of me?' he exclaimed. It was true that May Day was a celebratory date of great antiquity, reaching back to the pagan fire festival of Beltane, which marked the start of the summer. On this day, it was the custom for ordinary people to go into the country and gather green boughs in order to spend the day 'in triumph and pastime'.[33] Perhaps this did not strike quite the right note and a roistering crowd could never be absolutely trusted to do the right thing. So the Council chose 3 May, unaware that in the Catholic Church this was the Feast of the Invention (or Finding – from *invenire*, the Latin word for discovery) of the Holy Cross by the British Princess Helena. It was a feast to which Father Garnet had a particular devotion.

Despite Garnet's condemnation, the interrogations did not cease, nor did the concentration on the subject of equivocation. The day after the trial, Garnet made a new statement by which he hoped to clear up the Tresham affair. 'In cases of true and manifest treason a man is bound voluntarily to utter the very truth and in no way to equivocate', unless he knew about the treason by way of confession. In this case he was bound to seek all lawful ways to uncover the treason so long as the seal of the confessional was not broken. A few days later he wrote a letter to the King, protesting that he had been 'ever of the opinion' that it was unlawful to attempt any violence against the King's Majesty and the state, 'after he was once received by the realm'. When the government informed Garnet – a quite unequivocal lie – that they had captured Tesimond, Garnet took the opportunity to write his fellow priest a long letter apologising for the information he felt he must give away concerning Tesimond's walking confession.[34]

This letter, which was of course read – although Garnet was unaware of the fact – is the fullest account of what actually happened on that summer's day in the garden 'at the house in Essex' the previous year. Garnet maintained strongly to his fellow priest that everything had been told to him in confession, including as they walked 'because it was too tedious [painful] to hear all kneeling'. As for the Powder Treason, 'we both conspired to hinder it... I never approved it, nor, as I think, you'.

Although Waad in the Tower continued to insist that this so-called confession had in fact been nothing of the sort, the Jesuit never gave up. 'I took it as confession,' he said on one occasion, 'even if wrongly.' It would of course have suited the government's book to have eliminated this tiresome matter of Garnet's priestly oath of silence and to have concentrated on his treachery, pure and simple. This they never managed to do. The most Garnet ever conceded – somewhat dazed, and with the possibility at least of renewed torture – was this: 'If it [the news of the conspiracy] were not in confession, he conceived it to be delivered in confession.' There the irreconcilable matter rested.

Garnet's last letter to Anne Vaux was dated 21 April. He had already taken his leave of her and concerned himself with the various alternatives for her future in an earlier letter. This final missive was full of anguish, beginning: 'It pleaseth God daily to multiply my crosses.' Garnet hoped that God would grant him patience and perseverance to the end, as he related the various disasters which had occurred – first, his capture 'in a friend's house', then the confessions of the priests to each other and their secret conferences overheard at the Tower. After that, Tesimond had been captured (this was of course not true). Lastly, 'the slander of us both' – Garnet and Anne Vaux – had been spread abroad: this was all too true. Garnet concluded with a few lines in Latin which referred to the sufferings of Job. He signed himself: 'Yours *in eternum*, as I hope, HG.' Beneath the signature, he appended a rough drawing, a cross and the letters 'IHS' – the first three letters of the holy name of Jesus in Greek.[55]

CHAPTER SEVENTEEN

Farewells

Farewell, good friend Tom, this day I will save thee a
labour to provide my dinner.

FATHER HENRY GARNET
3 May 1606

Father Henry Garnet said his farewells in the Tower very
early on the morning of Saturday 3 May. King James was
no longer in London. The royal interest in the theological
arguments aroused by Henry Garnet's trial had waned in
favour of the other great kingly passion, the chase. James had
left for Newmarket in Suffolk on the Friday, hunting his way
happily northwards. Sir William Waad was left in charge of
delivering his prisoner, as he had been in charge of delivering
the conspirators in January.

The Jesuit, who had by now spent nearly three months as a
prisoner in the Tower, said a courteous goodbye to those who
had served him. To one of the cooks who called out, 'Farewell,
good sir,' he attempted a mild jest: 'Farewell, good friend Tom,
this day I will save thee a labour to provide my dinner.' Even
his captors were visibly moved. Lady Waad, well aware of what
lay ahead, told him that she would pray for him, adding: 'God
be with you and comfort you, good Mr Garnet...'¹

At the last moment, as Garnet, wearing a black cloak over
his clothes and a hat, was being strapped to the hurdle which
would take him to his death, there was a commotion in the
courtyard. A woman rushed forward. It was Anne Vaux.

It was in fact an administrative mistake that she should have been let out of her prison for this harrowing moment. Waad had given instructions that Mistress Vaux should be permitted to watch the priest's departure at a window. But her keeper allowed Anne right out into the courtyard itself, where the wicker hurdle lay with its burden. Anne was however dragged away before she could exchange one last word with her mentor, or even utter a prayer over the man who for twenty years had been the centre of her world.[2]

Evidently the patriotic protests of Sir Arthur Gorges, who thought the site of St Paul's Churchyard holy to the memory of Queen Elizabeth, had been disregarded, for this was the place chosen for the execution. The hurdle was drawn by three horses all the way from the Tower. Father Garnet lay on it with his hands held together and his eyes closed; he had the air of 'a man in deep contemplation'.[3] An enormous crowd awaited him at St Paul's. A scaffold had been erected on the west side for the prisoner, and there were wooden stands set up for spectators. The surrounding windows were also packed with onlookers.

Not all of them, of course, were hostile. At least one priest was present in disguise, hoping to perform the last rites on Father Garnet's moribund body, as Garnet in the past had done for others. This priest spent twelve pence for a seat on the stand and, as a result, he was able to supply Father Gerard later with numerous details for his *Narrative*.[4]

A Protestant account described Father Garnet as looking guilty and fearful at the prospect of his final ordeal, but in fact his main problem, once he had left the hurdle, was to secure any kind of repose in which to prepare himself for death.[5] The Sheriff of London was present, as were Sir Henry Montague, the Recorder of London, the Dean of Winchester, Dr George Abbot, and the Dean of St Paul's, Dr John Overal. In their different ways, all these gentlemen were determined to secure the last-minute repentance and even the conversion of this notorious Jesuit. It might be thought that someone who had already endured so much for the sake of his Church was unlikely to desert it at the end: but even in the last weeks in the Tower Garnet had been subjected to various doctrinal debates – in all of which of course he remained firm in favour of the Catholic Faith.

The Jesuit dealt quite easily with the request, made by the Recorder in the name of the King, to reveal any further treasons of which he had secret knowledge. He had, said Garnet, nothing more to say on that subject. But when the divines set about arguing with him about the superior merits of Protestantism, the priest 'cut them off quickly', asking them not to trouble themselves – or him: 'he came prepared and was resolved'. Garnet then desired some place apart where he could pray.[6]

This was not to be. Montague stated his orders were that Garnet should acknowledge himself justly condemned, and then seek the King's forgiveness. Garnet replied that he had committed no treason or offence against the King. They could condemn him for nothing except for keeping the secrets of the confessional: this was the only way in which he had had 'knowledge of that Powder Treason'. However, Garnet added, if he had indeed offended the King or the state, he asked for forgiveness with all his heart.

These last words encouraged the Recorder to believe he had secured the vital admission he wanted. He called out to the crowd to pay attention: the Jesuit had just asked for the King's forgiveness for the Powder Treason. But Garnet refused to accept this and he repeated that he was not guilty. The same open disagreement then took place on the controversial subject of Catesby, and Tesimond's confession to Garnet. Once again the priest refused to be browbeaten into giving way.

'You do but equivocate,' exclaimed Sir Henry Montague, 'and if you deny it, after your death we will publish your own hand [writing], that the world may see your false dealing.'

'This is not the time to talk of equivocation,' answered Garnet. 'Neither do I equivocate. But in troth,' he went on and then reiterated it: '*in troth*, you shall not find my hand otherwise than I have said.' This solemn declaration, made twice over, impressed the spectators. The Recorder's own reputation was not enhanced when Garnet demanded to inspect the famous document in his own writing. Montague had to reply, somewhat foolishly, that he had left it at home.[7]

When Garnet was asked – according to custom – whether he had anything further to say, he apologised for his own weakness, including his failing voice. But he did call attention to the appropriate date on which he was to die: 'Upon this day is recorded the Invention [Finding] of the Cross of Christ, and upon this day I thank God I have found my cross...' Although Garnet continued to deny his own guilt, he did take the opportunity to express once more his horror at the fact that Catholics had planned such an enterprise. In the future, he directed all Catholics to remain 'quiet', possessing their souls in peace: 'And God will not be forgetful of them.'

At this point, someone standing in the crowd near by shouted out: 'But Mr Garnet, were you not married to Mrs Anne Vaux?' The accusation stung Garnet, in a way nothing else could.

The priest turned to the people, and answered: 'That honourable gentlewoman hath [suffered] great wrong by such false reports. For it is suspected and said that I should be married to her, and worse. But I protest the contrary... she is a virtuous good gentlewoman and, therefore, to impute any such thing into her cannot proceed but of malice.' Having delivered himself of this broadside, Garnet was at last allowed to pray – at the foot of the ladder he would shortly mount.[8]

He himself assisted in the stripping off of his clothes down to his shirt; this was very long and Garnet had had the sides sewn up almost to the bottom in the interests of modesty 'that the wind might not blow it up'. One more Protestant minister did come forward, but Garnet refused to listen to him, or even acknowledge his presence. On the ladder itself, he paused and made the sign of the Cross, desiring all good Catholics present to pray for him. However one member of the crowd had evidently been assured that there would be a dramatic last-minute conversion to Protestantism (a government-inspired rumour).

This disappointed person shouted out: 'Mr Garnet, it is expected you should recant.'

'God forbid,' he replied. 'I never had any such meaning, but ever meant to die a true and perfect Catholic.'

This aroused a protest from Dr Overal, the Dean of St Paul's: 'But Mr Garnet, we are all Catholics.' But this the Jesuit would not have, as for him there was only one Catholic Roman Church, and that was under the Pope.[9]

Henry Garnet was now ready. He prayed for the welfare of the King and the Royal Family. Then he made the sign of the Cross. His last prayers were in Latin, the language of the 'one' Church into which he had been born and in whose service he had spent his life. They included 'Into thy hands, O Lord, I commend my spirit', uttered several times, and 'Mary, Mother of grace, Mother of mercy, protect us from the enemy, and receive us at the hour of our death.' This was the last prayer he said before he was told that the hangman was ready. The priest crossed his arms over his breast – it had not been thought necessary to bind his arms – and 'so was cast off the ladder'.

Then an odd thing happened. Many of the spectators had deliberately made their way to St Paul's in order to see a spectacle which included drawing and quartering performed upon a living body. But the mood of the fickle crowd suddenly changed. A great number of those present – they cannot all have been Catholics – surged forward. With a loud cry of 'hold, hold', they stopped the hangman cutting down the body while Garnet was still alive. Others pulled on the priest's legs, something which was traditionally done by relatives in order to ensure a speedy death. This favour was not something the crowd had chosen to perform for the conspirators in January, even though these had been 'men of good sort', popular and much esteemed. As a result Father Garnet was 'perfectly dead' when he was finally cut down and taken to the block.[10]

Even the traditional words 'Behold the heart of a traitor' received no applause. Nor did anyone cry out, 'God save the King' as was customary. Instead, there was an uneasy murmuring among the spectators.

*

That same day, 3 May, Father John Gerard, who had himself been named in the January proclamation, managed at last to get away from England to the continent and safety. He believed he owed his preservation to the intercession of the martyred Father Garnet. Gerard planned to make the crucial Channel crossing among the attendants of two envoys, Baron Hoboken and the Marquis de Germain. Hoboken represented the Archdukes and had been summoned to hear complaints concerning Hugh Owen and Father Baldwin in Flanders. The Marquis had, ironically enough, come from Spain to congratulate King James on surviving the Gunpowder Plot. However, these 'high officials' took fright at having such an incriminating presence in their midst. But at the last moment, as Gerard believed, 'Father Garnet was received into heaven and did not forget me.' The officials changed their minds, and the Marquis de Germain came in person to help Gerard into the livery which would enable him to pass as one of his entourage. 'In my own mind,' Gerard wrote, 'I have no doubt that I owed this [reversal of decision] to Father Garnet's prayers.'[11]

Father John Gerard lived on for over thirty years after the death of his friend and colleague; he died in Rome in his early seventies. Like Father Tesimond, also named in the proclamation, who had escaped a few months earlier in that cargo of dead pigs, Father Gerard lived to write a full *Narrative* of the events of the Powder Treason, many of which he had experienced first hand, while meticulous researches among survivors filled in the gaps. In 1609 when he was at the Jesuit seminary in Louvain, he wrote an *Autobiography*, which gave an account of his missionary life in England. It has been suggested by his editor and translator (both books were written in Latin) Father Philip Caraman that Gerard in conversation with the novices must have frequently told 'anecdotes of hunted priests, of torture and everyday heroism of his friends among the English laity'. Someone then suggested to the General of the Jesuits that all this would make an inspiring if distressing record.[12]

Anne Vaux also lived for another thirty years, despite the ill-health and bad eyesight which had dogged her throughout her life. She was released from the Tower in August 1606, about the same time as her servant James Johnson was let go (although the intention with Johnson seems to have been to let him act as a decoy to lead the authorities to recusant safe houses). Shortly after her release, a priest mentioned that Anne Vaux was 'much discontented' that she had not been allowed to die with Garnet. He added discreetly on the subject of her work and health: 'I believe the customers [the priests] and she will live together, but I fear not long.' His forecast was however incorrect, for Anne Vaux proved to be one of those dedicated people in whom a strong vocation prevails over a weak physique.[13]

At first, with her sister Eleanor Brooksby, Anne remained in London, presumably to fulfil Father Garnet's last instructions to lie low until matters had quieted down (although Anne did suffer another spell in prison for recusancy in 1608). The sisters then moved to Leicestershire, where they continued to harbour and protect priests, their names appearing together on recusant rolls from time to time until Eleanor's death in 1626. Anne's toil over decades was acknowledged by at least two dedications in works by eminent Jesuits, translated into English, one of which, by Leonard Lessius, printed in St Omer in 1621, had the appropriate title of *The Treasure of Vowed Chastity in Secular Persons*...[14] She never gave up her work for the 'customers'. In 1635, the year of her death at the age of seventy-three, her name was reported to the Privy Council for harbouring a Jesuit school for the education of young English Catholic gentlemen at her mansion, Stanley Grange, near Derby.

It was Anne Vaux, in the early stages of her grief at the death of Father Garnet, who was responsible for nurturing the story of a miraculous straw-husk bearing his martyred image. She was, wrote one who knew her, 'sometimes too ardent in divine things' – although the priests she protected over so many years would not have agreed.[15]

The story of the straw-husk began with the usual desperate search for holy mementoes among those Catholics covertly present, after the death of Father Garnet. One of these was a young man called John Wilkinson who had been asked by a fellow recusant, Mrs Griffin, a tailor's wife, to procure her some kind of relic. Wilkinson was therefore standing right by the hangman as he deposited Garnet's severed head in the usual straw-lined basket. All of a sudden an empty husk of corn stained with the priest's blood 'did leap… in a strange manner' into his hand. Wilkinson gave the husk to Mrs Griffin, who put it in a crystal reliquary.[16]

There were two versions as to when the bloodstain revealed itself to bear 'the proportion, features and countenance of a pale, wan dead man's face' perfectly resembling Father Garnet, with his eyes closed, beard bespotted with blood and a bloody circle round his neck. Father Gerard heard that the image had been perceived by Mrs Griffin with a mixture of fear and joy, after three or four days. Another story linked the husk to the equally miraculous whiteness of Father Garnet's features, visible once his head was hoist on its pole by London Bridge. Although these heads were customarily parboiled (which made them black), Father Garnet's pallor was so remarkable as to cause general wonder. It also attracted a crowd of spectators, to the extent that after six weeks the government had to order the face to be turned upwards away from the inspection of the curious. According to this second (anonymous) account it was at this point that the likeness appeared in the corn-husk.

The husk in its reliquary was a natural focus of devotion among the faithful – including Anne Vaux who was shown it in the course of the autumn – and curiosity among the rest. As a counterpoint to the comfort the husk gave to the bereaved Catholics, it caused the English government and its representatives abroad considerable irritation. Sir Thomas Edmondes complained about a reproduction of the image being circulated in Brussels, and the Archduke Albert managed to have a book on the subject of the straw-husk suppressed. Sir Charles Cornwallis, however, had less success with Philip III in Spain. He did not manage to get pictures of 'Henry Garnet, an English man martyred in London' censored, even though they

Farewells

were specifically designed to show up the King of England as a
tyrant.[17]

Zuñiga, the Spanish Ambassador in London, was in fact
among those who inspected the straw-husk. He did so, as he
told Philip III, 'from curiosity' after hearing about the husk
from several sources, although he denied that he had paid for
the privilege, being 'never such an enemy to my money as to
give it for straws'.[18] In actual fact, the husk was probably concealed at the Spanish Embassy for a while, before being smug-
gled abroad. There it found a place among the relics in the
possession of the Society of Jesus, before disappearing in the
general turmoil of the French Revolution.

Like her sister-in-law Anne, Eliza Vaux of Harrowden maintained her fidelity to the recusant cause for the rest of her life.
She was released from her house arrest in London in April
1606 after a series of protests at her condition, made with characteristic vigour. Free to live at Harrowden once more, she
continued to harbour priests, Father Percy taking the place of
Father Gerard as her chaplain. In 1611, however, she was
arrested once again and Harrowden was ransacked, owing to a
rumour (untrue) that Father Gerard had returned to England.
The next year Eliza Vaux was indicted at the Old Bailey for
refusing to take the Oath of Allegiance, and condemned to
perpetual imprisonment in Newgate. In July 1613, she was
released on grounds of ill-health; she died about twelve years
later without ever deserting the Faith which she had proudly
chosen, and admirably served.[19]

Eliza had done her best for the family of six children which
had been her responsibility following the early death of her
husband. The eldest, Mary, had married Sir George Symeon of
Brightwell Baldwin in Oxfordshire in 1604; the youngest,
Catherine, became the second wife of George Lord
Abergavenny ten years later. The middle daughter, Joyce,
became a nun in the recently founded Institute of the Blessed
Virgin Mary and, dying in 1667, outlived all the family. After
the suppression of the order by the Pope, 'Mother Joyce' spent
her declining years at Eye in Suffolk, living with her brother

137

Henry.[20] Neither of Eliza's younger sons, Henry and William, married. It was the marital career of Eliza's eldest son Edward Lord Vaux which provided a strange, one might even say romantic, footnote, to the events of November 1605.

Edward's projected marriage to Lady Elizabeth Howard had been blighted by the discovery of the Powder Treason, and soon after Elizabeth had been married off to Lord Knollys, later the Earl of Banbury, forty years her senior. For a quarter of a century Edward himself did not marry. Then in 1632, he finally married his erstwhile sweetheart, Elizabeth Countess of Banbury, six weeks after the death of her aged husband.

Their love had evidently not been in abeyance all that length of time for Elizabeth, who bore no children to Lord Banbury for many years, gave birth to two sons in 1628 and 1630 respectively. These boys were widely supposed to be the offspring of Lord Vaux rather than Lord Banbury (who was by then over eighty). It was a view which Edward Vaux's testament only encouraged. Being theoretically without issue, he left Harrowden to his wife Elizabeth on his death, in remainder to her elder son, Nicholas, second Earl of Banbury. Unfortunately – if not altogether surprisingly – Nicholas' inheritance of the Banbury earldom was itself the subject of a long lawsuit, which, after Nicholas' death, his own son and heir Charles continued with zest.* The result was that Harrowden itself had to be sold in 1694, to meet the legal costs.[21]

So the house in which Edmund Campion and John Gerard had been hidden was replaced by the present structure by the new owner Thomas Watson-Wentworth in the early eighteenth century. It is surely legitimate to regard Edward Vaux and Elizabeth Howard as indirect victims of the Powder Treason, since, given their enduring passion for each other, they must surely have enjoyed a long and happy marriage had they been allowed to wed in November 1605.

The mothers, wives and children of the conspirators were not

* The present (10th) Lord Vaux of Harrowden descends in the female line from Mary Vaux, Lady Symeon, the eldest sister of Edward, 4th Lord Vaux.

coated with social ignominy, but they were, according to custom where traitors' families were concerned, pursued with financial vengeance. Guy Fawkes of course left no descendants to suffer, no widow and no children. He died as he had lived since the distant days of his Yorkshire childhood, a soldier of fortune to outsiders, but to himself a latterday crusader, whose strongest allegiance was to the Church in whose honour he planned to wield his sword.

Robert Catesby's mother Anne – deprived of a farewell as her son lurked in the fields by Ashby St Ledgers – was left trying to rescue something from the wreckage. She concentrated on holding on to her own marriage settlement from Sir William Catesby, for the benefit of her grandson, also named Robert. Lady Catesby was successful, as the settlement was not finally disturbed, despite the best efforts of the crown. But the younger Robert left no descendants, and, for better or worse, the direct Catesby line from the notorious conspirator died out.*[22]

Lady Catesby's sister, Muriel Lady Tresham, who had similarly mothered a traitor in Francis Tresham – or at any rate one whom the government treated as such – faced the same problem of trying to salvage the Tresham estate. Unlike Lady Catesby, Lady Tresham still had three unmarried daughters needing portions (eight of her eleven children had survived infancy, which was an astonishingly high proportion for the late sixteenth century). Then there was the need to maintain Francis' widow Anne and her small children. Although, as has been noted, the entail upon male heirs saved the Tresham estate from the worst effects of the attainder – Francis Tresham had no son – all Lady Tresham's gallant efforts were vitiated by the financial irresponsibility of Francis' brother Sir Lewis Tresham (he acquired a baronetcy in 1611). In the shadow of the 'Catholic Moses', as Sir Thomas Tresham had been known, his sons had grown up reckless and selfish,

* The Catesby family, kin to Robert but not descended from him, is however flourishing today. The famous eighteenth-century naturalist Mark Catesby, author of *Natural History of Carolina, Florida and the Bahama Islands* (1731), was part of it.

inheriting their father's extravagance but not his moral strength, nor his grandeur. Already in difficulties before he inherited in 1605, Sir Lewis managed to complete the ruin of the family, and with the death of his son William in 1643 the Tresham baronetcy came to an end.[23]

Eliza Tresham, daughter of Francis, married Sir George Heneage of Lincolnshire. But her sister Lucy Tresham carried out her father's 'earnest desire', expressed on his deathbed, that one of his girls should become a nun. Taking the name of Mother Winifred – an allusion, no doubt, to St Winifred of Holywell, to whom recusants had so much devotion – Lucy Tresham lived her life out in St Monica's at Louvain, a new-founded convent in the Low Countries.[24] While in one sense she was far away from the tumults of English Catholicism, in another sense she was only one among many women in these convents who had connections to the Gunpowder Plot.

There were already twenty-two English nuns, Canonesses Regular of the Lateran, at St Ursula's, Louvain, in 1606, the year in which its offshoot St Monica's was founded. Father Garnet's sisters, Margaret and Helen, who had been professed at St Ursula's in the late 1590s, were among the first to move to St Monica's. Alongside them, Lucy Tresham found herself enjoying what Father Garnet had called 'that most secure and quiet haven of a religious life', in a letter to his sister Margaret.[25] Dorothea Rookwood, half-sister of Ambrose, was also there, and Mary Wintour, daughter of Robert and Gertrude, was professed in 1617.

One cannot help speculating about whether the subject of the Powder Treason was ever discussed in the convent refectory and, if so, in what terms. One can at least be sure that the most fervent prayers for the dead were offered on 3 May, the anniversary of Father Garnet's death. There were further connections and, one may assume, further prayers for the dead. Mary Ward, founder of the Institute of the Blessed Virgin Mary, was the niece of the Wright brothers, Jack and Christopher; Joyce Vaux and Susanna Rookwood, a further half-sister of Ambrose, were two of her earliest and closest associates.

The continued courageous and devout adherence to Catholicism was one thing that the families of the conspirators had in common after the event. Another daughter of Robert and Gertrude Wintour, Helena, was noted for her splendid gifts to the Jesuits,* while a son, Sir John Wintour, was 'a noted Papist' in the English Civil War. It is not absolutely clear whether Kenelm and John Digby, the sons of Sir Everard, were raised as Catholics after his death, since sources vary. But certainly the dazzling Sir Kenelm Digby – writer, diplomat, naval commander, lover and finally husband of Venetia Stanley – would describe himself in a memoir as a Catholic by the time he reached twenty, when he was living in Spain. It is likely that his devout mother had ensured a kind of covert Catholic instruction and influence all along, even if forbidden by law to bring up her sons in her own religion.[26]

Even the six children of Lord Monteagle, who had professed his new Anglican loyalties to King James, followed the religion of their pious Tresham mother, who remained a recusant. His eldest son Henry Lord Morley (the title which Monteagle inherited from his father in 1618) was a Catholic peer in the reign of Charles I. Monteagle was not at first disposed to grant the request of his eldest daughter Frances Parker, who was physically handicapped, to become a nun. But he finally surrendered, 'in respect that she was crooked, and therefore not fit for the world'. He gave her a handsome dowry of a thousand pounds.[27]

If the Catholic strain remained, the strain of dissidence and bravado appeared to vanish – with one exception. Ambrose Rookwood, great-grandson of the conspirator, was named for him – an ill-omened name, one might have thought, and so it proved. After the Restoration, Ambrose rose in the Stuart army to become a brigadier under James II. Unfortunately he preserved his Jacobite sympathies following the ejection of the

---

* Vestments, embroidered by her, including a set of white High Mass vestments of which the chasuble bears the words 'Ora pro me Helena Wintour', are still to be seen at the Jesuit-run Stonyhurst College, Clitheroe, in Lancashire (see plate section).

Catholic James from the throne in favour of his Protestant son-in-law and daughter, William and Mary.

In 1696 Brigadier Rookwood was involved in a plot to assassinate King William. When one of his co-conspirators turned King's evidence he was apprehended (in a well-known Jacobite ale-house) and taken to Newgate prison. After being tried for high treason, Ambrose Rookwood was put to death at Tyburn on 29 April 1696 – the second man of that name within the century to die for the ultimate offence. But Ambrose Rookwood the younger did not exhibit at the last quite the noble spirit of his ancestor; in a paper he delivered at the scaffold, he declared that he had only been obeying the orders of a superior officer.[28]

The Catholic peers who had been arrested at the time of the discovery of the Plot were subjected, like the conspirators' families, to a process of political forgiveness – provided they paid up. Lord Montague, who should somehow have known better than to employ a young Yorkshireman called Guy Fawkes as his footman fifteen years previously, was one who had always spoken up fearlessly for 'the ancient Faith'. At the moment of the Plot's discovery, he was questioned on the subject by his father-in-law, the powerful and venerable Lord High Treasurer, the Earl of Dorset. Montague expressed his absolute horror at such an undertaking and still further shock at the very idea that he, Montague, could be involved. 'I never knew what grief was until now,' he told Dorset. Montague also asked his father-in-law's advice on how he could get back into the King's good graces without violating the integrity of his religious principles. The short answer was, of course, money. Montague paid a fine and he also underwent a spell of imprisonment. Thanks to Dorset's influence, however, he escaped trial.[29]

His grandmother Magdalen Viscountess Montague, now in the evening of her life, certainly did not allow anything – including frequent searches of her establishments around the festivals of the Church such as Easter – to violate the integrity of her Faith: a Faith which she had held since her youth, when she had been Maid of Honour to Queen Mary Tudor. This representative of the grand old, unswervingly loyal Catholicism, whose prayers had been sought by Queen Elizabeth, died in 1608 at her house near Battle. There had been no less than five priests in the house to say Mass the day before, and William Byrd wrote an elegy to mark her death.[30]

Lords Mordaunt and Stourton were not so fortunate as Montague. Both Catholic peers – one connected to Robert Keyes, the other Francis Tresham's brother-in-law – faced trial in front of the Star Chamber, and were condemned to imprisonment in the Tower. In 1608 they were transferred to the Fleet prison. Lord Mordaunt was fined ten thousand pounds, although it is not clear whether the money was ever handed over, since his son was 'forgiven' the fine in 1620. Lord Stourton was fined six thousand pounds but was finally allowed to settle for paying a thousand.[31]

Meanwhile Monteagle, the other Tresham brother-in-law, enjoyed the pension granted to him for his heroic role in discovering the conspiracy, and he otherwise occupied himself with his interest in colonial enterprises. He donated to the second Virginia Company and was elected a member of its council in 1609, and he had shares in the East India and North-West Passage companies. However, it has to be said that his executors complained that his pension was in arrears to the tune of nearly two thousand pounds at his death in 1622.[32]

At least Monteagle used his influence to protect his brother-in-law Thomas Habington from the ultimate consequences of harbouring the forbidden priests at Hindlip, which could have been death. Although Habington was condemned, the pleas of his wife to her brother secured his reprieve. So he survived to pursue his antiquarian interests with vigour for the rest of his long life. Thomas Habington died in 1647 at the age of eighty-seven, his enthusiasm, as with Anne Vaux, leading to longevity. The baby William Habington, who had been born at Hindlip on the inauspicious day – from the Catholic point of view – of

5 November 1605, survived this traumatic birthdate to become a poet, author among other works of *Castara*. He estimated his own work as 'not so high as to be wondered at, nor so low as to be condemned'. Many recusants of the previous generation would have been happy to have been so judged.[33]

In political and personal terms, the clear loser from the affray of the Powder Treason was the Earl of Northumberland. Nothing was ever proved against him: none of the Plotters, tortured or self-preserving, confessed his name as the putative Protector; nor did the Jesuits incriminate him in the course of their overheard conversation. Salisbury was riding high at the time of Northumberland's trial in front of the Star Chamber in June 1606, having been made a Knight of the Garter in April.* Even he admitted that Northumberland would never have let those he loved perish in the explosion: a man of 'his birth, alliance and disposition'. It seems, therefore, to have been the personal distrust of the King which cast a fatal blight upon Northumberland.[34]

What caused this distrust? The indictment charged Northumberland with 'endeavouring to be the head of the English Papists, and to procure them Toleration'. The admission of Thomas Percy to the ranks of the King's bodyguards without causing him to take the Oath of Supremacy, knowing him to be a recusant, was cited as proof. This was a charge with which Coke was able to make merry, in his usual style, when he described the promotion of Percy to such an intimate position as putting 'an axe in his hand to carry it over the King's head'. There was also Northumberland's interest in the matter of the King's horoscope, and how long he would reign.[35] Northumberland's patronage of Thomas Percy was an ineluctable fact, and he admitted to the treasonable affair of the horoscope (although since the chart had – quite correctly – predicted a long reign for James I, it is difficult to see that much damage had been done).

---

* Although there were rumours that the lofty Kings of France and Denmark had protested at this, considering a Cecil too common for such an honour, Salisbury was installed a fortnight after Garnet's death.

But it was surely the question of toleration and, above all, those promises made (or not made) by the King while still in Scotland which were the key element in James' distrust of Northumberland. Coke himself summed it up when he said that the King himself had given his royal word (*in verbo regio*) that 'he never did promise or command' toleration.[36] Whatever the truth was of those distant dealings – whether Thomas Percy lied then or the King was lying now – it was wrapped in a convenient Scottish mist which obliterated all memories of such a very different era. It was Northumberland who in 1606 paid the penalty for being the front man of the Catholics, a position from which, in 1603, he had hoped to reap the reward.

At his trial, Northumberland, who was hampered by his deafness (he had of course no counsel), was fined thirty thousand pounds, and sentenced to imprisonment at the King's pleasure. He kept increasingly magnificent state during his incarceration. In the capacious Martin Tower he had a study, library, great chamber, withdrawing-room and two dining-rooms; while his personal cook (he was not reliant on Father Garnet's 'good friend Tom') lived in a rented house on Tower Hill. His accounts show not only considerable expenditure on clothing, but also that he was in the habit of wearing the blue ribbon signifying his membership of the Order of the Garter, since it frequently had to be renewed.[37] Nevertheless Northumberland remained in the Tower until 1621, when his son-in-law, the King's favourite Lord Hay, successfully pleaded for his release. He retired to his estate at Petworth, where he died in 1632.

The government had pinned down Northumberland for his part in the conspiracy, but those 'Plotters' abroad who were the bane of the English government's existence remained happily outside the long arm of its law. The Archdukes did not keep Hugh Owen long under house arrest and no charges were brought against him. When Owen moved on to Spain, Salisbury tried in vain to get him kidnapped and brought to England. However, Hugh Owen retired to Rome with a pension and lived to the age of eighty. That old soldier – and old intriguer – Sir William Stanley also lived on in freedom to the age of eighty. Only Father William Baldwin, the Cornish priest who had been named in the indictment of January 1606 as being part of the conspiracy, fell into the English net, although not for some years. The Archdukes had declined to extradite him then, but in the course of a journey to Rome in 1610 Baldwin was captured by the Protestant Elector Palatine, who despatched him to England. He remained in the Tower until 1618, even though no charge of treason was ever brought against him, presumably for lack of evidence. Father Baldwin's final release was due to the intervention of the Spanish Ambassador. He was then banished, and thereafter he spent eleven years as Rector of the English seminary at St Omer.[38]

Spared from destruction by gunpowder, the Royal Family, that domestic phenomenon still new to the English in 1603, was surely set to prosper. Where religion was concerned, Anne of Denmark maintained the discreet stance with which she had handled the difficult months following the discovery of the treason. The more or less public Catholicism on which the Pope and others had pinned so many hopes while she was still in Scotland (and which had deluded them about James' own Catholic sympathies) gave way to something more elegantly lethargic. In 1612 Pope Paul V would even go so far as to refer woundingly to the Queen's 'inconstancy'. In view of the many changes she had made in religious matters, he wondered if it was even true that she was a Catholic. Anne of Denmark *was* certainly a Catholic – she fitted up a chapel at her palace at Oatlands, and enjoyed having Catholic priests come to minister to her at Hampton Court.[39] But from 5 November 1605 onwards she lived her life as a royal version of a Church Papist. Like Church Papists in the reign of Elizabeth she wanted spiritual consolation in private, but no trouble in public.

There was however a fleeting quality to this perceived prosperity of the Royal Family, and May 1606, when Father Garnet on the scaffold prayed for its welfare, turned out to be the

high point of its expansion. There were then four living children, two Princes and two Princesses, and the Queen was on
the verge of giving birth yet again. But the expected baby, who
was born on 22 June and named Sophia, died the next day.[40]
Then Princess Mary, the special child because she had been
born in England following her father's accession, died in
September 1607 at the age of two and a half.*

No treasonable horoscope would have dared to predict that
the glorious Prince of Wales would be the next to die. Prince
Henry had been the hope of the nation ever since he won all
hearts at the first royal procession of the reign. Alas for such
expectations: he died of typhoid fever at the age of eighteen in
November 1612. That left his brother Prince Charles, that
timid, undersized child known to the conspirators as the Duke
of York. He succeeded James in 1625 as King Charles I.

If the death of the healthy upstanding Prince Henry would
have been an unlikely prediction for anyone in England in
1606, the execution of Charles I, by his own subjects in 1649,
would have been an unthinkable one. The roundabout of
history turned again. Nicholas Owen's cunningly devised
hiding-places, designed to protect Catholic priests from the
government of James I, enabled James' grandson Charles II to
elude capture after his defeat by Cromwell at Worcester.
Subsequently, the throne of England was lost to the male
Stuarts. For all the seeming fecundity of the Stuart dynasty, the
seventeenth century was destined to draw to a close exactly as
the sixteenth century had done: with problems of succession
and religion compounded by the reigns of two childless sisters
– Mary II and Anne. On the death of Queen Anne in 1714,
the Protestant succession passed as it had done in 1603 to a
foreigner, the Elector George of Hanover.

King George I was the great-grandson of James I. His right
to the throne was derived from his maternal grandmother.
There is a delicate irony in the fact that this grandmother was

* She was buried, like the infant Princess Sophia, in Westminster Abbey. Poignant
monuments to them both can be seen in the North Aisle of the Henry VII
Chapel (see plate section).

none other than the Princess Elizabeth, that little girl whom the Gunpowder Plotters had intended to place upon the throne as their puppet monarch, and marry off to some suitably Catholic prince. A staunch Protestant all her life, even at the early age of nine, the Princess had once regarded with horror the prospect of receiving the crown in this unnatural manner. With the ripeness of time, however, the crown did come the way of her posterity. Indeed, it is the direct descendant of this same Princess Elizabeth, mooted in 1605 as sovereign in her own right, who sits upon the throne of Great Britain today as Queen Elizabeth II.

So the *dramatis personae* of the Powder Treason and of their descendants made their farewells, dead, fled or reintegrated in their different ways into English life. But the propaganda war was only just beginning.

CHAPTER EIGHTEEN

Satan's Policy?

The quintessence of Satan's policy, the furthest reach and stain of human malice and cruelty, not to be paralleled... as I am persuaded, among the more brutish cannibals.

FRANCIS HERRING
Popish Pietie, 1610

Nearly four hundred years have passed since that dark night in November when searchers found a 'desperate fellow' with explosives in the vaulted room beneath the House of Lords. In the time that has elapsed, the Gunpowder Plot has meant many different things to many different people – including many different historians. The propaganda war has been long and vigorous and shows no signs of abating, given that the most recent scholarly works on the subject have taken diametrically opposite points of view.

Father Francis Edwards, S.J., in *Guy Fawkes: the real story of the Gunpowder Plot?* (1969), maintains that the entire conspiracy was devised by Robert Cecil, Earl of Salisbury, hereditary foe to the moderate English Catholics, who used double-agents including Robert Catesby himself (deliberately killed at Holbeach to stop his mouth), Guy Fawkes and Thomas Percy. Mark Nicholls in *Investigating Gunpowder Plot* (1992) believes that 'it is surely more realistic to see the treason as one of the greatest challenges that early modern state-security ever faced...'[*1]

---

* The argument looks fair to continue, since Father Edwards has returned to the attack in 'Still Investigating Gunpowder Plot', *Recusant History* (1993), a review of Nicholls' book countering his arguments.

These two totally irreconcilable positions have in fact been present in the historiography of the Gunpowder Plot from the very beginning. Taking the government's official stance first, its invective on the subject (including the vituperative language of Sir Edward Coke) was based on the premise of an appalling danger narrowly averted. Succeeding writers and pamphleteers built energetically upon these foundations in what came to be a prolific body of literature. An extract from a work of 1610 entitled *Popish Pietie* by a physician named Francis Herring is a characteristic reflection of it, rather than an exaggerated version of the genre. For Herring, the Powder Treason – 'that monstrous birth of the Roman harlot' – was 'the quintessence of Satan's policy, the furthest reach and stain of human malice and cruelty, not to be paralleled among the savage Turks, the barbarous Indians, nor, as I am persuaded, among the more brutish cannibals'.[2]

In such estimates, there was an additional *frisson* in the status of the proposed victim. A King – God's chosen representative on earth – had been menaced. That meant that the conspiracy was not only wicked but actually sacrilegious. *Macbeth*, first performed in 1606 (possibly at Hampton Court in August to mark the state visit of Queen Anne's brother King Christian of Denmark),* is a work redolent with outrage at the monstrous upsetting of the natural order, which is brought about when subjects kill their lawful sovereign.

> O horror! horror! horror!
> Tongue nor heart cannot conceive, nor name thee!

Macduff's appalled cry when he discovered the bloodstained body of the murdered King Duncan would have certainly reminded his hearers in that summer of 1606 of the recent conspiracy against their own King. Macduff's words of

---

* Although this may have been a shortened version. Scholarly disputes on the dating of *Macbeth* agree at least on one thing: that the inspiration of the Porter's scene must have followed the trial and execution of Father Garnet. See *Macbeth* (Muir), pp. xv–xxv, for a discussion of the play's dating.

shocked expostulation even echoed the government indictment against the conspirators, which found the Gunpowder Plot to be a treason such as 'the tongue of man never delivered, the ear of man never heard, the heart of man never conceived ...'.[3]

Rumours concerning the King's safety – a monarch who was once threatened in such an appalling manner could always be threatened again – continued to rustle in the nervy months following the discovery of the Plot. At the end of March a story spread that James had been stabbed by a poisoned knife at Okingham, twenty miles from London, 'Which treason, some said, was performed by English Jesuits, some by Scots in women's apparel, and others by Spaniards or Frenchmen' (showing an even-handed list of contemporary prejudices).[4] The story was a complete fantasy, but it demonstrated the continued perturbation on the subject of the King's personal safety; he was 'the life o'th' building', as Macbeth described Duncan, whose presence guaranteed order.

The Papists' Powder Treason, an allegorical engraving done for 5 November 1612 'in aeternal memory of the divine bounty in England's preservation from the Hellish Powder Plot', was careful to glorify the King, as the central feature of what had been preserved. A series of royal portraits, including Prince Henry and Princess Elizabeth, loom over much smaller vignettes of Monteagle receiving the anonymous letter from a stranger and the conspirators taking their sacramental oath. It was unfortunate that the divine bounty failed the next day, when Prince Henry died of his fever on 6 November. The engraving had to be withdrawn (although it emerged in 1679, another period of virulent anti-Popery).*[5]

Such perturbation, personalised and focused on King James, was grist to the government's mill in its campaign against the treacherous Catholics. First, these traitors paid allegiance to the Pope rather than to their King; then, their perceived leaders,

---

* A painted version of this engraving hangs in New College, Oxford, today (see plate section); it was commissioned and donated by a physician named Richard Haydocke, who probably had a hand in the design, and maybe in the painting as well (Weller, *passim*).

the Jesuits, were actual 'King-killers'. A rhyming pamphlet of 1606 on the subject of the Powder Treason by the playwright Thomas Dekker contains 'The Picture of a Jesuit':

> A Harpy face, a Fox's head …
> A Mandrake's voice, whose tunes are cries,
> So piercing that the hearer dies,
> Mouth'd like an Ape, his innate spite
> Being to mock those he cannot bite …[6]

Like Francis Herring's disquisition on 'Satan's policy', this violent caricature was not atypical of the way Jesuits were portrayed henceforth. Not only were they 'King-killers', but they were also equivocators.

The doctrine of equivocation continued to be seen, like the Jesuits themselves, as at once alien and diabolical. In *Macbeth* Shakespeare began by amusing himself on the subject, when the drunken Porter of Macbeth's castle, awakened by knocking, imagined that he was at Hell's Gate, welcoming the new arrivals. His language recalled the popular gibes made on the subject of Garnet's death, including that jocular remark by Dudley Carleton to his correspondent John Chamberlain that Garnet would be hanged without 'equivocation' for all his shifting and faltering.* 'Faith, here's an equivocator,' exclaimed the Porter, 'that could swear in both the scales against either scale; who committed treason enough for God's sake, yet could not equivocate to heaven: O! come in, equivocator.'[7]

Towards the end of the play, a more serious use of the word occurred. Macbeth began to suspect that 'the equivocation of the fiend' was responsible for two comforting prophecies which had been made to him. One Apparition, summoned by the witches, had told him: 'Fear not, till Birnam Wood comes to Dunsinane'; the other Apparition had assured him that 'none of woman born shall harm Macbeth'. But Birnam Wood

---

* Another knocker at Hell's Gate – 'a farmer, that hang'd himself on th' expectation of plenty' – may also be a reference to Garnet, since Farmer was among his many aliases, those 'appellations' listed by Coke as evidence of deceit.

did advance on Dunsinane – in the shape of Macbeth's enemies disguised as branches – and Macduff did have the power to kill him, being 'from his mother's womb untimely ripp'd'.[8] Both prophecies were classic examples of equivocation, since Macbeth had understood them in one sense, while their hidden (sinister) meaning turned out to be very different.

This use of equivocation was seen as an essentially evil process: 'a monster shapeless, two-headed, two-horned, and also with a double mouth, and especially a double heart', as William Gager described equivocation in *Pyramis*, a Latin poem of 1608 dedicated to the King.[9] It was a shapeless mythical monster that bore little relation to the actual Catholic doctrine of equivocation – heroic if arguably ill-advised – which was intended to avoid the sin of lying when in dangerous conditions.

Such propaganda accompanied the political measures taken by the government after the discovery of the Plot, and provided the correct climate for persecution. Much of this was directed at the blameless Catholic community, exactly as Father Garnet and others had feared. The Catholics, like the Protestants, trembled in the wake of the Plot, fearing a general massacre of their number inspired by a spirit of 'vengeance and hatred'.[10]

In April 1606 Henri IV of France decided to give King James a little lecture on the virtues of toleration – and who better to do it than the man who had changed his religion to secure a kingdom? 'His master had learned from experience', said the French Ambassador in London, 'the strong hold which religion has on the human breast' (if not perhaps on Henry IV's own); it was a flame which tended to burn with increasing fierceness in proportion to the violence employed to extinguish it. Let King James, therefore, punish the guilty, but let him equally spare the innocent.[11] These same admirable sentiments had in fact been expressed by James himself in his speech to Parliament of 9 November 1605. Now he saw things differently.

The King told the French Ambassador that the English

Catholics 'were so infected with the doctrine of the Jesuits, respecting the subordination of the royal to the papal authority', that he could do nothing. He would leave it to his Parliament. So another Oath of Allegiance was devised, with help from an Appellant Catholic priest, intended to increase the rift between those priests prepared to 'compromise' with the state, such as the Appellants, and those who could not, the Jesuits. It was an oath which resulted in a long propaganda war between King James and the defenders of the Pope's spiritual supremacy.[12] But from the point of view of the hapless recusants, such doctrinal wars were less important than the disabilities which came to burden their daily lives.

As these disabilities multiplied, Catholics could no longer practise law, nor serve in the Army or Navy as officers (on pain of a hundred pounds fine). No recusant could act as executor of a will or guardian to a minor, nor even possess a weapon except in cases of self-defence. Catholics could not receive a university degree, and could not vote in local elections (until 1797) nor in Parliamentary elections until Catholic Emancipation in 1829. All this was on top of the spiritual penalties by which Catholics were ordered to marry in the Anglican Church, take their children there for baptism, and finally rest in its burial ground.

In 1613 a bill was introduced into the House of Commons to compel Catholics to wear a red hat (as the Jews in Rome did) or parti-coloured stockings (like clowns did), not only so that they could be easily distinguished, but also so they could be 'hooted at' whenever they appeared. Wiser counsels prevailed and this unpleasant scapegoating was not carried through. Nevertheless a profound prejudice against Papists, with or without red hats and parti-coloured stockings, remained lurking in the popular consciousness after 1605, ready to emerge from its depths at any hint of leniency towards them. For many Protestants, a declaration of February 1606 on the subject of the Plot by Sir Thomas Smith summed the matter up: 'this bloody stain and mark will never be washed out of Popish religion'.[13]

It was a stain which could be passed on to unborn genera-tions. It was the allegedly 'foreign' nature of Catholicism – ruled by an alien Pope based in Rome – which made it peren-nially vulnerable to attack. A political organisation could be denounced where genuine religious convictions might evoke sympathy. In 1651 Milton called Catholicism not so much a religion as 'a [foreign] priestly despotism under the cloak of religion arrayed in the spoils of temporal power'.[14] He was on firm ground that would not be surrendered by every Protestant until the late twentieth century (if then). Meanwhile, as the contents of the anniversary sermons on 5 November reveal, the notion of a conspiracy which was so frightful as to be directed by Satan himself only deepened with the passing of the years.

Was the Plot really 'Satan's policy' – that is, the work of Satan carried out by the Catholics? Or was some other agency responsible, rather closer to the King? The first rumours that the mastermind was in fact Salisbury, not Satan, occurred in November 1605. As early as 17 November, the Venetian Ambassador, Niccolò Molin, reported: 'people say that this plot must have its roots high up'. Another cynical account described the fire which was to have 'burnt our King and Council' as being but '*ignis fatuus* [will o' the wisp] or a flash of some foolish fellow's brain'.[15]

Such stories suited the Catholic powers abroad, because they shifted the embarrassing responsibility for the conspiracy away from their own co-religionists (Philip III, for example, on first hearing the news had hoped that Puritans would turn out to be involved). On 25 November Sir Thomas Edmondes in Brussels told Salisbury that he was ashamed to repeat the 'daily new inventions at this court' which were intended to exonerate the Catholics from scandal. An anonymous letter of December held it as certain that 'there has been foul play', that some members of the Council had spun the web which had embroiled the Catholics.[16]

Not only were rumours of foul play convenient for the Catholic powers, they also offered (and still offer) the most convenient defence for those reluctant to face the fact that convinced, pious Catholics could also be terrorists. Bishop Godfrey Goodman's memoir *The Court of King James the First*, written about forty years after the event, provided material for this approach, albeit of a somewhat flimsy nature (the whole memoir has little scholarly quality). Goodman was the son of the Dean of Westminster and rose to become Bishop of Gloucester, despite being suspected of holding 'papistical views'. His special interest was in fact the reconciliation of the Anglican Church and Rome, which he described in his will as the 'mother church'.[17]

Goodman made Salisbury the clear villain of the piece. He began by drawing attention to the Catholics' acute feelings of grievance after the death of the 'old woman' (Queen Elizabeth) when they did not receive 'the mitigation' that they had expected. Salisbury's intelligence service had let him know all about this, whereupon he decided that in order to demonstrate his service to the state, 'he would first contrive and then discover a treason' – the more odious the treason, the greater the service. Thus Percy was an *agent provocateur* who was 'often seen' coming out of Salisbury's house at 2.00 a.m. Salisbury was meanwhile giving specific instructions for the convenient deaths of Catesby and Percy: 'Let me never see them alive.' But Goodman produces no proof for any of this, beyond second-hand gossip.

Nevertheless the sheer seductiveness of the story – from the Catholic point of view – prevented its dying away completely. In 1679, when the imaginary Popish Plot of Titus Oates created new waves of anti-Popery, Thomas Barlow, the fiercely anti-Catholic Bishop of Lincoln, saw fit to publish a fresh work on the Gunpowder Plot, which he called that 'villainy so black and horrid ... as has no parallel in any age or nation'. However, in the course of his narrative, Barlow also found it necessary to denounce the persistent 'wicked' rumours about Salisbury's role. The Plot, he reiterated fiercely, had been 'hatched in Hell' by the Jesuits.[18]

Of course Salisbury himself never tried to conceal the fact

that he had had knowledge of some impending 'stir'. He not only mentioned it in his official communication to the English ambassadors but told King James, who repeated it in his own account of the Plot. The reputation of Salisbury's intelligence service demanded no less and it would have ill become the King's chief minister to plead total ignorance of such a flagrant conspiracy under his very nose.

Salisbury's penetration of the Plot is one thing but the deliberate manufacture of the entire conspiracy with the aim of damning Catholicism for ever is quite another. There is far too much evidence of treasonable Catholic enterprises in late Elizabethan times for the Gunpowder Plot to be dismissed altogether as malevolent invention. It was, on the contrary, a terrorist conspiracy spurred on by resentment of the King's broken promises. The wrongs of the persecuted Catholics were thus to be righted by the classic terrorist method of violence, which encompassed the destruction of the innocent as well as the guilty.

The story told here has been of Salisbury's foreknowledge – at a comparatively late stage – thanks to the revelations of Francis Tresham repeated to Monteagle and his subsequent manipulation of the King by the stratagem of the anonymous letter. This limited foreknowledge makes sense of the extraordinary ten-day delay in searching the House of Lords for gunpowder – otherwise quite incomprehensible in a responsible and security-minded minister. In his Cold War against the forces of Catholicism, Salisbury scented the opportunity for a coup, particularly when it turned out that he could very likely entangle the hated Jesuits in the same net.

But foreknowledge is not fabrication, even if Salisbury, or perhaps Coke, did embellish the truth with certain vivid details afterwards, such as the celebrated – and infamous – mine which somehow vanished without trace. In the same way, the very different foreknowledge gained by Father Garnet, in the confessional, did not mean that he was, as Coke tried to suggest, the principal 'author' of the Plot. Neither Salisbury nor Father Garnet was the author of the Powder Treason, though both have been blamed for it. There is, however, a real difference between Salisbury and Garnet in that Salisbury gained by the Plot and Garnet suffered for it.

Could the Gunpowder Plot have succeeded? For it is certainly true that regimes have been triumphantly overthrown by violent means throughout history. If Salisbury's foreknowledge, albeit limited, is accepted, one must also accept that these conspirators never really had a chance once the Plot was in its last stages. Tresham's betrayal and Monteagle's eye to the King's preservation (and his own) saw to that, quite apart from Salisbury's industrious intelligence system.

But Salisbury's loyal activities, like the decisions of Tresham and Monteagle, were symptoms of a wider failure which was built into the scheme long before the last stages were reached. For the Gunpowder Plot to succeed, the conspirators needed to be sure of strong support at home and even stronger support abroad. King James understood the first point perfectly well, and expressed it eloquently when he said that the traitors had been 'dreaming to themselves that they had the virtues of a snow-ball' which would begin in a small way, but by 'tumbling down from a great hill' would grow to an enormous size, gathering snow all the way.[19]

In fact the snow-ball, far from increasing as it went, melted away in the light of the Plot's discovery. The Catholic community, whatever resistance it might have provided in the time of Elizabeth, had been cozened to believe that James, the son of the Catholic Mary Queen of Scots, would act as its deliverer once he ascended the throne. By the time the truth was discovered – James did not intend to keep the promises they thought he had made – it was too late. Two sorts of Catholic leaders, the peers and the priests, never gave encouragement to the violence of the Powder Treason.

Any support abroad had vanished as a genuine possibility even before the death of Elizabeth. It vanished when the King of Spain, for all his diplomatic dallying, refused to back a specific Catholic candidate for the English throne (such as his sister Isabella – herself in any case a reluctant nominee).

Thereafter the Anglo-Spanish Treaty confirmed the gloomy fact that there was to be no help from that quarter. Once again the Hapsburg – and Papal – belief in the impending Catholicism of King James was relevant. The King bamboozled two sets of Catholics into compliance by his slippery handling of his own religious convictions: English recusants and foreign potentates, including the Pope.

Quite apart from the continuing battle between Pro-Plotters and No-Plotters, the conspiracy has developed a rich historiographical life of its own. One feature of this has been the concentration on the figure of Guy Fawkes. It is Guy Fawkes who has had to accept the odium of being the arch-villain of the piece. William Hazlitt, in an essay of 1821 to commemorate 5 November, described him as 'this pale miner in the infernal regions, skulking in his retreat with his cloak and dark lanthorn, moving cautiously about among his barrels of gunpowder, loaded with death…'[20] It is Guy Fawkes who, in spite of having been generally known in his own time, including to the government, as Guido, has lent his forename to the stuffed, ragged figures on the pavement, whose placard solicits 'a penny for the guy', before being ritually burnt on 5 November. In all fairness, the reviled name should really be that of Robert Catesby, as leader of the conspiracy. But it may be some consolation to the shade of Guido, if it still wanders somewhere beneath the House of Lords, that Guy Fawkes is also the hero of some perennial subversive jokes as being 'the only man to get into Parliament with the right intentions'.

In memory of the failed endeavour of Guy Fawkes, the vaults of the House of Lords are still searched on the eve of the Opening of Parliament. The practice has become one of the many rituals which accompany and enhance British political procedures, connecting them to a vivid past. But the search has its origins in genuine panic about the Catholic menace. Nearly thirty-six years after the discovery of the Gunpowder Plot, the alleged massacres of Protestants by Irish Catholics aroused these fears. On 18 August 1641, Parliament, which was in a ferment over these supposed atrocities, believed that the threat might have moved closer to home. Orders were given to search 'Rosebie's House, the Tavern, and such other Houses and Vaults and Cellars as are near the Upper House of Parliament' for powder, arms or ammunition.[21]

A similar panic marked the period surrounding Titus Oates' revelations of a Popish Plot in 1678. In late October, the House of Lords was told by the Gentleman Usher of the Black Rod that coals and timber had been lodged in the cellars adjoining and that, even worse, 'a great knocking and digging' in the earth had been heard there. Seventy years after the Powder Treason, with Catholics still very much the prime suspects, this was enough to raise the alarm. The House of Lords set up a committee, which was to have the cellars cleared of firewood, so that sentinels, under the command of trusted officers, could patrol these dangerous areas day and night. A certain Mrs Dehaure, living in the Old Palace Yard, was ordered out of her home so that it could be filled with guards.[22]

Again in 1690, following the accession of William III, there were fears of Jacobite insurrection on behalf of the exiled Stuarts. The Marquess of Carmarthen reported to the House of Lords that there was strong cause to believe that there was 'a second Gunpowder Plot, or some such great Mischief', since notorious 'ill-wishers' were resorting to the house of one Hutchinson in the Old Palace, Westminster.[23] Nor were these fears totally imaginary. The assassination plot which led to the execution of Ambrose Rookwood the second occurred only six years later.

In the calmer weather of the eighteenth century, the search became progressively ritualised. In 1760 an agreeable new piece of ceremony was introduced, as is demonstrated by the accounts of a wine-merchant named Old Bellamy who was allowed to rent the vaults. The searchers ended their search by drinking the loyal toast in port which he supplied. By 1807 it had become the regular practice, supported by custom, for 'The Lord Chamberlain of England' to make a search for 'combustibles' under or near either House of Parliament before its Opening. After the fire which demolished much of the Palace of Westminster, Bellamy's wine-shop moved to nearby Parliament Street – but happily the custom of port-drinking continued.[24]

From the beginning of the twentieth century, a detachment of ten men of the Queen's Body Guard of the Yeomen of the Guard was accustomed to perform the search just before the Opening of Parliament by the sovereign and it still does. The Yeomen of the Guard, in their splendid scarlet uniforms and black Tudor hats, carrying lanterns, weave among the large modern pipes which heat the Palace of Westminster. Port is still drunk at the end of the search (after a lapse, the custom was revived, but without the loyal toast, in 1976).[25] So far as is known, however, the one successful search ever made – in the sense that perilous substances and a perilous person actually turned up – occurred on the night of 5 November 1605.

A second feature of the historiography of the Gunpowder Plot has been the attention paid to the date itself, variously known as Guy Fawkes Day and Bonfire Night.* Unlike many English celebrations, 5 November was not invented by the Victorians with their talent for conjuring up instant, rich, immemorial traditions. Nor for that matter are its origins lost in antiquity, linked over centuries to the Celtic fire festival at the beginning of winter (which later merged into the Catholic Feast of All Saints also on 1 November). As David Cressy has written in his study of the subject, there has been 'much speculative nonsense' floated along these lines: the English Bonfire Night comes directly from the date of the Opening of

* It is the day, not the year, which has proved '*utterly* and even maddeningly MEMORABLE' in the words of W. C. Sellar and R. C. Yeatman's *1066 and All That* (1930, pp. 62–3). It would be fair to say that there are many able to mutter:

> Please to remember the Fifth of November
> Gunpowder Treason and Plot
> We know no reason why Gunpowder Treason
> Should ever be forgot

(in one of its many variations) who, if challenged, would not be able to name the actual year in which these memorable events took place.

Parliament in 1605, and the proximity to 1 November is purely coincidental.*[26]

Nevertheless this emphasis on the day itself has, like the opposing arguments, been present since the beginning. The first bonfires were lit on 5 November 1605 itself, the first sermon preached soon after. An analysis of the Gunpowder sermons (those preached on the anniversary) shows a concentration on the day which is almost mystical in its fervour. In 1606 Bishop Lancelot Andrewes preached from the text 'This is the day which the Lord hath made; let us rejoice and be glad in it.' He went on, 'The day (we all know) was meant to be the day of all our deaths...It is our Passe-over,' and made an even more solemn comparison to the Day of Resurrection. Altogether Andrewes, a fervent preacher of King James, would preach ten Gunpowder sermons. In 1618 he summed up the national feeling of patriotism mixed with religion: 'Here we have the making of a new Holy-day (over and above those of God's in the laws).'[27]

Predictably enough, celebrations waxed or waned according to the waves of anti-Catholicism which periodically shook England. Any apparent support given to that dangerous foreign-based religion, any renewed threat from its supporters, was enough to make the annual bonfires burn brighter. The marriage of Charles I to a French Catholic princess, the so-called Popish Plot of 1679, the Catholicism of James II – how convenient that his supplanter William III landed in England on 5 November! – all these events met with outbursts of conflagration.[28]

Yet there was one element present in the celebrations of the anniversary which would need diplomatic handling as the years passed. The original 5 November had been a date of royal deliverance: essentially it was a monarch who had been saved from destruction. Yet in 1647 – two years before the execution of Charles I – Parliament abolished all feasts *except* the 5 November celebration, on the ground that the day stood for

---

* It will be recalled that this date was changed twice: the last postponement was from 3 October. According to Cressy's argument, we might well have been chanting 'Please to remember the Third of October'.

the foiling of Papists, regardless of its other implications. Fifth of November continued to be celebrated under the Commonwealth, the only national feast to survive. This was despite a certain illogicality in commemorating the saving of a King from destruction by a people who had recently put their own King to death.[29]

Still stranger, in a sense, was the transmutation of Bonfire Night after it had crossed the Atlantic. Here were men and women who had come, very many of them, to throw off the chains of royalist absolutism: it might be questioned whether the annual memory of an English King's deliverance was really such an appropriate occasion for rejoicing. If celebrating a royal anniversary was too negative, the answer was to emphasise the positive: that is, to burn a Pope of Rome, still in charge, rather than Guy Fawkes, long vanished. Thus Pope Day, a rumbustious occasion of mob revelry and mob rivalries, came to be celebrated, mainly in New England, on 5 November. It was a special feature of Boston life among the 'lower elements', but spread as far south as Charleston.[30]

Increasingly, there was something anarchic about the occasion, with strong anti-governmental undertones, particularly so long as that government was British. During the struggles for American Independence, advantage was taken of the flexibility inherent in Pope Day (or Bonfire Night) when the effigy of any displeasing person could be burnt so long as that of the Pope went along too. Not everyone joined in the revelry: the custom was condemned by George Washington as 'ridiculous and childish'. Notwithstanding, Lord Bute, George III's Prime Minister, began to feature. In 1774, in Charleston, the Jacobite Pretender to the throne (Bonnie Prince Charlie), the Pope and the Devil all shared a bonfire with English tea. In another contemporary bonfire Lord North was burnt, wearing his Star and Garter, as well as Governor Hutchinson, once again accompanied by the Pope and the Devil. When an effigy was burnt in 1780 of Benedict Arnold, the turncoat American general who joined the British side, it was a symbolic protest which bore very little relation to the original 5 November celebration.[31]

So the bonfires of Pope Day died down, the celebration lingering on in the nineteenth century in places like Newburyport, Massachusetts, and Portsmouth and New Castle in New Hampshire mainly as an occasion for a boisterous outing for children, asking for money. Those in Newburyport who chanted, 'Here is the Pope that we have got / The whole promoter of the Plot,' had very little, if any, idea of the historical significance of what they were saying. In the United States, the coincidental proximity of 5 November to Hallowe'en on 31 October (to say nothing of the great national feast of Thanksgiving, roughly three weeks later) has meant that few folk memories of it survive, let alone celebrations, except among those of recent British descent, or with special British connections.*

In the Old World, as opposed to the New, Guy Fawkes Day was far from vanishing away. A study of popular prints on the subject of religion from 1600 up till 1832 shows anti-Catholicism and the political connotations of Popery as one theme that spans the whole period. The prayer of thanksgiving on 5 November remained in the Anglican Book of Prayer until 1859.† Protestant pastors annually remembered the hideous fate designed for King and Royal Family 'by Popish treachery appointed as sheep to the slaughter'. As they intoned, 'From this unnatural conspiracy not our merit but Thy mercy, not our foresight but Thy providence delivered us,' it was made clear that the unnatural conspiracy had been the work of *the* Catholics, not just a small group of them.[32]

This stubborn sense of Catholic menace did however mean

* Widespread enquiries by the author in 1993–4 failed to produce information concerning any indigenous celebration of 5 November in the United States – that is, festivals with continuity to the seventeenth century and Pope Day. All those who did mark Guy Fawkes Day in one form or another were careful to emphasise that their rituals were purely enjoyable and had absolutely no connotation of anti-Catholicism: as one correspondent wrote: 'much more Dionysian than anti-papal'.

† It was discontinued along with the official commemoration of two other days of monarchical significance, 30 January (execution of Charles I, 1649) and 29 May (restoration of Charles II, 1660).

that Guy Fawkes Day itself moved away, as in the United States, from the notion of royal deliverance. It moved in the direction of rowdy popular demonstrations on the one hand and anti-Popery on the other. Typical of the rowdy aspect was the running battle in Exeter, extending over forty years, between a popular force known as 'Young Exeter' and the authorities. In the course of it a High Churchman and right-wing Tory was burnt in effigy for his opposition to the Reform Bill in 1832.[33]

As for anti-Popery, the restoration of the Catholic hierarchy in 1850 was marked by the burning of the effigies of the new Catholic Archbishop of Westminster, Cardinal Wiseman, along with the Pope and certain Jesuits, on 5 November. For his part, Cardinal Wiseman protested against people being invited 'to feast their eyes upon the mock execution of individuals' (expressing the distaste that many have always felt for such practices).* At least Catholic priests in England could thank God 'that their effigies and not their persons' were in the hands of those who had made the effigies and lit the bon-fires.[34]

This was not an exaggerated reaction, given the bursts of anti-Catholicism which continued to erupt publicly even in places where wiser counsels might have been expected. The publication of David Jardine's *A Narrative of the Gunpowder Plot* in 1857 merely stirred the controversy further. For Jardine placed a full measure of blame upon the Jesuits, with Garnet 'a willing, consenting and approving confederate'. He also made a thinly veiled accusation that certain documents condemning the Jesuits had been suppressed.[35]

In this way William Turnbull, a Scottish Catholic archivist working in the Public Record Office, became embroiled in the controversy as the supposed author of this suppression. Extreme Protestants – led by the rabidly anti-Catholic Tory

* One Catholic schoolmaster, Dom. Antony Sutch O.S.B. of Downside, used to celebrate 6 November as opposed to the 5th, as a protest against such practices: on this day he recalled to his pupils the sufferings of the Elizabethan and Jacobean Catholic martyrs (information supplied to the author).

MP for Warwickshire North, Charles Newdigate Newdegate –
howled for his resignation. In vain the Master of the Rolls,
Lord Romilly, issued a public statement which totally excul-
pated Turnbull. Newdegate, who also issued wild accusations
of treason against Cardinal Manning, had his way. Turnbull
resigned in 1861 and died, broken by the experience, not long
after. Certainly the Gunpowder Plot cast a long shadow.[36] One
of Newdegate's additional motives in his campaign of enmity
was to smear his Liberal political opponents in Warwickshire
who happened to be Catholics: the Throckmortons of
Coughton Court.

The immolation of current hate-figures – in effigy – was the
way Guy Fawkes Day was to go from the eighteenth century
onwards. It was, after all, a fertile field, and remains so. Joan
Courthope was the daughter of a late-nineteenth-century
Sussex squire. When she was thirteen, she recorded in her diary
angry British feeling concerning the Boer leader 'Oom Paul'
Kruger at the outset of the Boer War. On 5 November 1899,
at Ticehurst, a suitable effigy having been constructed, the
march 'The Downfall of Kruger' was played and a large
bonfire was lit. At the end, Joan noted laconically, 'Kruger
chucked in.'[37]

A hundred years later, the most famous Bonfire Night celebrations in England, those of Lewes in East Sussex, also con-
centrate, merrily enough, on burning the infamous – or just the
famous. In 1994 effigies included Mrs Thatcher, John Major on
a dinosaur taken from the film *Jurassic Park*, and the Home
Secretary Michael Howard in the week of the publication of
the unpopular Criminal Justice Bill, as well as Guy Fawkes
himself. The celebrations were attended by an estimated eighty
thousand people, with two thousand of them marching.[38]

The town festival has a long history – anti-Catholicism was
encouraged by the fact that seventeen Protestant martyrs were
burnt there under Queen Mary Tudor – and in 1785 the Riot
Act had to be read, owing to the conspicuous violence of the
crowd. Nowadays there are five rural Bonfire Societies, whose

members adopt various forms of historical fancy dress for their contests. Only one of them, however, the Cliffe, still burns an effigy of the Pope. (But the Cliffe is careful to make it clear that it is a seventeenth-century Pope which is being burnt, not the present incumbent.) An apt comparison can be made to the Palio in Siena with its similar loyalties and rivalries. In short, Lewes now provides 'a night of wildness and fun' rather than something more sinister, although there will always be those who will be made uneasy by the sight of the words 'No Popery' on a banner slung across an English street, let alone the burning of the Pope – any Pope – in effigy.* Perhaps those, including the present writer, who recoil from such sights, should take comfort from the sensible words in an American colonial almanac of 1746:

> Powder-plot is not forgot
> 'Twill be observed by many a sot.[39]

All these ebullient and on the whole light-hearted festivities have little connection to the serious men who plotted the downfall of the government in 1605. The courage of the Powder Plotters is undeniable and even those hottest in condemning their enterprise have paid tribute to it. A notable example of this is provided by the historian S. R. Gardiner, locked for many years in the late nineteenth century in a Pro-Plot versus No-Plot controversy. He even expressed a certain satisfaction that so many of the original conspirators cheated the scaffold by their doomed last stand at Holbeach. 'Atrocious as the whole undertaking was,' he wrote, 'great as must have been the moral obliquity of their minds before they could have conceived such a project, there was at least nothing mean or selfish about them. They had boldly risked their lives for what they honestly believed to be the cause of God and their country.'[40]

---

* The Catholic parish priest at St Pancras, Lewes, since the mid-1980s, whose church is passed by the bonfire processions, emphasises that he has not found Lewes to be an anti-Catholic town in any way.

In their own times this was understood, even by those – Catholics – who disapproved in principle of any such adventure based on the destruction of the innocent. Father John Gerard, in his *Narrative*, compared the conspirators (his intimate friends) to the Maccabees, the Jewish warriors who delivered their people from the Syrians in the second century. 'Seeing members of their brethren to suffer patiently the unjust oppression of their adversaries', the Maccabees decided that if everyone was similarly passive 'they will now quickly root us out of the earth'.* The comparison was an apt one as this was in essence the stance expressed by the conspirator Robert Keyes at his trial, when he spoke little but 'showed plenty of spirit'. Keyes thought it the lesser of two evils 'to die rather than live in the midst of so much tyranny'.[41]

It is not a position that the world can expect to see abandoned so long as the persecution of minorities – and for that matter of majorities – survives. Terrorism after all does not exist in a vacuum. 'I do not, however, deny that I planned sabotage. I did not plan it in a spirit of recklessness or because I have any love of violence. I planned it as a result of a calm and sober assessment of the political situation that had arisen after many years of tyranny, exploitation, and oppression of my people...' These are not the words of Robert Catesby, but *mutatis mutandis* they could in fact have been uttered by him had he lived to defend his actions to the world. This is in fact the speech, three hundred and fifty years later, of Nelson Mandela, in the dock for his leadership of the African National Congress, at the Rivonia Trial of 1964: he chose to quote it in his autobiography *The Long Walk to Freedom* as an explanation but not an excuse.[42]

Mandela was sentenced to life imprisonment (and served twenty-five years) before he was elected President of South Africa in 1991. In the end, President Mandela was not, therefore, to be one of the myriad 'defeated' human beings to whom 'History', in the lines of W. H. Auden on the Spanish

---

* The Maccabees decided (unlike their brethren) to fight on the Sabbath day: 'let us not all die as our brethren died in their hiding-places' (1 Maccabees 2:40–1).

Civil War, 'may say Alas but cannot help nor pardon...' Yet this passage in his autobiography reminds us of one reason why terrorism, successful or otherwise, will probably always remain as the behaviour of last resort for some: 'The hard facts were that fifty years of non-violence had brought [my] people nothing but more repressive legislation, and fewer rights.'

The Gunpowder Plotters were terrorists and they were defeated. They were not good men – by no stretch of the imagination can they be described as that. The goodness in this tragic episode belongs to the priests and lay brothers such as Nicholas Owen (Little John) and the heroic women. But, under different circumstances, they might have been very differently regarded. One might go to the opposite extreme and represent the Plotters as brave, bad men: but perhaps brave, misguided men is a kinder verdict which may be allowed at this distance of time.[43]

The study of history can at least bring respect for those whose motives, if not their actions, were noble and idealistic. It was indeed a 'heavy and doleful tragedy' that men of such calibre were driven by continued religious persecution to Gunpowder, Treason and Plot.

Notes

Details of books, documents etc., given here in abbreviated form, will be found in
the list of Reference Books p. 181.

Chapter Eleven: Mr Fawkes Is Taken

1 S.T., II, pp. 197ff.
2 Coughton Court and the Throckmortons, passim.
3 Anstruther, Vaux, p. 281; S.T., II, pp. 232, 241; Tierney, IV, p. cii.
4 Morris, Gerard's Narrative, p. ccxxxvi.
5 King's History, S.T., II, p. 199.
6 Gardiner, Plot, p. 68.
7 C.S.P. Domestic, VIII, p. 246; Gardiner, Plot, p. 67.
8 Gerard, What Plot?, App. N, p. 276; Barlow, pp. 200ff.
9 Barlow, pp. 201–2; the Littletons are sometimes wrongly
  described as brothers; but see Nash, Worcestershire, I, p. 493;
  Edwards, Tesimond, pp. 132–3, note; Dures, pp. 42ff.
10 C.S.P. Domestic, VIII, p. 282; S.P. 14/216/178; Humphreys,
  'Wyntours', p. 74.

11 Gardiner, *Plot*, p. 68; but see H.M.C. Salisbury, XVII, pp. 509–10 for lines omitted.

12 Nicholls, pp. 163ff.

13 Nicholls, p. 158 note 70.

14 Batho, *Northumberland*, pp. 5–6; Nicholls, p. 153; H.M.C. Salisbury, XVII, pp. 529–30.

15 S.T., II, p. 199; H.M.C. Salisbury, XVII, pp. 481–2; Gardiner, *Plot*, p. 131.

16 There was a No-Plot suggestion that Whynniard *died* on 5 November: possibly eliminated by the government as a cover for its own conspiracy. This has recently been shown to be incorrect since he signed his last will three weeks later; see Nicholls, p. 216.

17 Larkin, p. 123.

18 Gardiner, *Plot*, p. 68.

19 Anstruther, *Vaux*, p. 307.

20 Gardiner, *Plot*, p. 68.

21 S.P. 14/216/22.

22 Nicholls, p. 43; Williamson, pp. 174ff.; Digby's examination, C.S.P. Domestic, VIII, p. 260; S.P. 14/216/94.

23 Stow, p. 879; Nicholls, p. 13.

24 Stow, p. 881.

25 Nicholls, p. 10.

26 Bodleian, Ashmole MS., 363, fol. 241; Thomas, p. 312; Larkin, p. 123.

27 C.J., p. 257.

28 S.T., II, p. 201.

Chapter Twelve: The Gentler Tortures

1 Edwards, *Tesimond*, p. 33; Shakespeare Trust, ER 27/14.

2 Nicholls, p. 11.

3 S.P. 14/216/18.

4 Coke, *Third*, p. 35; Jardine, *Torture*, p. 35; Edwards, *Tesimond*, p. 49 note.

5 Bellamy, pp. 120ff.

6 Cooper, p. 119; Jardine, *Torture*, p. 23ff.

7 Bellamy, p. 119; Read, p. 37.

8 Cooper, pp. 105–19.

9 S.P. 14/216/37.

10 Bellamy, p. 113.

11 Bellamy, p. 112; Lingard, VII, pp. 261–2 note 135.

12 Goodman, II, p. 106; Morris, *Gerard's Narrative*, p. 105; S.T., II, p. 218; C.S.P. Domestic, VIII, p. 292; Edwards, *Tesimond*, p. 129.

13 H.M.C. Salisbury, XVII, p. 479; Goodman, II, p. 106.

14 H.M.C. Salisbury, XVII, p. 479.

15 H.M.C. Salisbury, XVII, p. 479.

16 Jardine, *Torture*, pp. 2–5.

17 Larkin, pp. 124–6; S.P. 14/216/22.

18 C.S.P. Domestic, p. 288; Edwards, *Tesimond*, p. 153.

19 Caraman, *Garnet*, p. 330.

20 Anstruther, *Vaux*, p. 310.

21 Anstruther, *Vaux*, pp. 300–1.

22 Caraman, *Garnet*, p. 330.

23 Hamilton, I, pp. 182–3; S.P. 14/216/178; C.S.P. Domestic, p. 282.

24 Tierney, IV, pp. cxi–cxii.

25 Gardiner, *Plot*, p. 69; S.P. 14/216/135; C.S.P. Domestic, VIII, p. 265.

26 Humphreys, 'Wyntours', pp. 65ff.

27 S.T., II, pp. 186–7.

28 Gardiner, *Plot*, p. 69.

29 Williamson, p. 182.

30 Gardiner, *Plot*, p. 69; H.M.C. Salisbury, XVII, p. 531.

31 H.M.C. Salisbury, XVII, p. 486; Bodleian, Ashmole MS. 363, fol. 241.

32 H.M.C. Salisbury, XVII, p. 486.

33 Edwards, *Tesimond*, pp. 134–5; H.M.C. Salisbury, XVII, p. 486.

34 Making a quantity of 1,800 lb since the Ordnance Board used a short hundredweight of 100 lbs; P.R.O., W.O. 49/31/101; Rodger, pp. 124–5. It used to be suggested by No-Plotters that the records had been removed for some reason, but this has been demonstrated to be untrue.

35 Anstruther, *Vaux*, pp. 290–1.

36 C.S.P. Venetian, X, p. 325; Magee, p. 38; De Luna, p. 138; H.M.C. Salisbury, XVII, p. 480; Goodman, I, pp. 120–2.

37 S.P. 14/216/49; S.T., II, pp. 202–3; Gerard, *What Plot?*, App. N, p. 268.

38 S.P. 14/216/54.

Chapter Thirteen: Fire and Brimstone

1 *King's Book*; McIlwain, pp. 281ff.

2 C.J., p. 257; *King's Book*; McIlwain, p. 289.

Notes (pages 42–57)

3 Larkin, p. 125.
4 Edwards, *Fawkes*, pp. 190–1.
5 Hurstfield, *Freedom*, p. 327; Edwards, *Fawkes*, p. 191.
6 See Nowak, *passim*; D.N.B. Barlow.
7 Nowak, p. 48.
8 Loomie, 'Catholic Consort', pp. 306ff.
9 Nichols, I, p. 592.
10 H.M.C. Salisbury, XVIII, p. 68; Nichols, I, p. 591.
11 Edwards, *Tesimond*, p. 136.
12 H.M.C. Salisbury, XVII, p. 490.
13 C.S.P. Domestic, VIII, p. 250; Anstruther, *Vaux*, pp. 283–5.
14 Gerard, *Autobiography*, pp. 197–8; H.M.C. Salisbury, XVII, pp. 490–1.
15 S.P. 14/216/156; S.P. 14/216/226; C.S.P. Domestic, VIII, p. 249; Anstruther, *Vaux*, pp. 295–6; G.E.C. Teynham.
16 Gerard, *Autobiography*, p. 208.
17 Anstruther, *Vaux*, p. 327.
18 Edwards, *Fawkes*, p. 181.
19 H.M.C. Salisbury, XVII, p. 534.
20 H.M.C. Salisbury, XVIII, pp. 38–40; H.M.C. Salisbury, XVII, p. 534.
21 S.T., II, p. 170; Nicholls, p. 38.
22 D.N.B. Waad; Caraman, *Garnet*, pp. 348–9.
23 The handy short title by which the official account came to be known. The full title was *His Majesties Speach in this Last Session of Parliament… Together with a discourse of the maner of the discouery of the late intended Treason, ioyned with an Examination of some of the prisoners.*
24 H.M.C. Salisbury, XVII, p. 541.
25 S.T., II, p. 22.
26 Anstruther, *Vaux*, p. 308.
27 C.S.P. Domestic, VIII, p. 254.
28 H.M.C. Salisbury, XVII, p. 534.
29 Hatfield MS 113/54; S.P. 14/216/114; 'apparently altered by Coke to 25', H.M.C. Salisbury, XVII, pp. xvi, 509–10, 512–13; Gardiner, *Plot*, pp. 57 69; Nicholls, p. 28 and notes 50–3; Williamson, App. I, pp. 247–500; Devlin, *Hamlet*, p. 148.
30 Williamson, App. I, p. 248 and Plates II and IV; H.M.C. Salisbury, XVII, pp. 512–13.
31 H.M.C. Salisbury, XVII, p. 502.
32 H.M.C. Salisbury, XVII, pp. 509–10.
33 Shirley, pp. 336–40; C.S.P. Domestic, VIII, 1603–1610, p. 257.

173

34 H.M.C. Salisbury, XVII, p. 535.
35 Batho, 'Wizard Earl', pp. 344ff.
36 S.P. 14/216/136; C.S.P. Domestic, VIII, p. 266.
37 Edwards, *Tesimond*, p. 137.
38 Barlow, p. 200.
39 S.P. 14/216/145; C.S.P. Domestic, VIII, p. 267.
40 S.P. 14/216/166; C.S.P. Domestic, VIII, p. 279.
41 The presence of Foster makes nonsense of the theory that the government poisoned Tresham for knowing too much about their machinations; Wake, pp. 31ff.
42 Wake, pp. 33–4; H.M.C. Salisbury, XVII, pp. 528, 553.
43 H.M.C. Salisbury, XVII, p. 558; Wake, p. 34.
44 S.P. 14/216/211; Wake, p. 40.
45 Wake, p. 34.
46 Wake, p. 40.
47 Finch, p. 92; Williamson, p. 196.

Chapter Fourteen: These Wretches

 1 By 'J.M.', Harrison, *Jacobean*, p. 261.
 2 C.S.P. Venetian, X, pp. 308–9.
 3 Caraman, *Garnet*, p. 316.
 4 Anstruther, *Vaux*, p. 200; Edwards, *Tesimond*, p. 163.
 5 Larkin, p. 128; Humphreys, 'Wyntours', pp. 71ff.; H.M.C. Salisbury, XVIII, pp. 11–12.
 6 H.M.C. Salisbury, XVIII, p. 34; Edwards, *Tesimond*, pp. 164–5.
 7 Waugh, p. 18.
 8 Anstruther, *Vaux*, pp. 333–5; Humphreys, 'Wyntours', p. 52.
 9 Comment of an eye-witness, Anstruther, *Vaux*, p. 334.
10 Anstruther, *Vaux*, p. 334.
11 Morris, *Gerard's Narrative*, p. 153.
12 Anstruther, *Vaux*, p. 335.
13 Anstruther, *Vaux*, p. 190.
14 H.M.C. Salisbury, XVIII, pp. 35–6.
15 H.M.C. Salisbury, XVIII, pp. 34–5; S.P. 14/216/202; C.S.P. Domestic, VIII, p. 299.
16 Caraman, *Garnet*, pp. 339–40.
17 Caraman, *Garnet*, p. 339.
18 Edwards, *Tesimond*, p. 172; Anstruther, *Vaux*, p. 340.
19 C.J., pp. 257, 260; H.M.C. Montagu, pp. 47–9; D.N.B. Edward Montague.

20 Nichols, I, p. 590.
21 Anstruther, *Vaux*, pp. 132–3; Bellamy, pp. 9ff.; Carswell, p. 42.
22 Nichols, I, p. 35.
23 Somers, *Tracts*, XI, p. 113; Willson, p. 301.
24 S.T., II, pp. 159–64, 187.
25 S.T., II, pp. 164–6.
26 S.T., II, pp. 166–84.
27 Jardine, *Trials*, II, pp. 120–1 and note 2, 139 and note 2.
28 Jardine, *Trials*, II, p. 159 and note 1; Lingard, X, p. 44 and note 1.
29 S.T., II, pp. 185–7.
30 S.T., II, pp. 186–7.
31 S.T., II, p. 186.
32 S.T., II, pp. 187–8.
33 S.T., II, pp. 188–9.
34 S.T., II, pp. 189–94.

Chapter Fifteen: The Heart of a Traitor

1 H.M.C. Salisbury, XVIII, pp. 36–7.
2 Anstruther, *Vaux*, p. 339. It has been suggested that the government speeded up the executions in order to avoid confrontation with Father Garnet (still held captive in the midlands). But in fact executions at this period often did follow quickly upon convictions; see Bellamy, p. 182.
3 S.T., II, p. 182.
4 Barlow, pp. 197ff.
5 S.T., II, pp. 215–16.
6 Edwards, *Tesimond*, p. 226.
7 Wood, II, p. 241.
8 H.M.C. Salisbury, XVIII, p. 52; Edwards, *Tesimond*, p. 227.
9 Morris, *Gerard's Narrative*, p. 219; S.T., II, p. 182.
10 Morris, *Gerard's Narrative*, pp. 219–20.
11 S.T., II, p. 216.
12 S.T., II, p. 217.
13 S.T., II, p. 218; Morris, *Gerard's Narrative*, p. 221.
14 S.T., II, p. 218.
15 Humphreys, 'Habingtons', p. 57.
16 Morris, *Gerard's Narrative*, pp. 157–8.
17 Edwards, *Tesimond*, p. 175.
18 Hurstfield, 'Succession', p. 380; Gerard, *Autobiography*, p. 86; Anstruther, *Vaux*, p. 353.

19 Morris, *Gerard's Narrative*, p. clxxxix.
20 C.J., p. 264.
21 C.J., p. 265; C.S.P. Venetian, X, p. 321.
22 Caraman, *Garnet*, pp. 348ff.
23 Caraman, *Garnet*, pp. 350, 371, 422.
24 Gerard, *Autobiography*, p. 96.
25 Anstruther, *Vaux*, pp. 256, 347.
26 Anstruther, *Vaux*, p. 183.
27 C.S.P. Domestic, VIII, p. 263.
28 Morris, *Gerard's Narrative*, p. 172; Anstruther, *Vaux*, p. 186.
29 Caraman, *Garnet*, p. 351.
30 S.T., II, pp. 166–7.
31 Jardine, *Equivocation*, p. vii; Garnet, 'Equivocation', Bodleian, Laud MS., misc. 655, p. 1; Malloch, 'Garnet', p. 391; Allison, pp. 14–15.
32 Allison, p. 14; Malloch, 'Garnet', p. 387; Devlin, *Southwell*, App. C., pp. 333–5; Zagorin, pp. 12ff.; Holmes, *Resistance*, pp. 1ff.
33 Jardine, *Equivocation*, p. 3; Foley, VII, p. 1358.
34 Jardine, *Equivocation*, p. vii.
35 Basset, p. 135; Zagorin, p. 195.
36 Rose, pp. 80ff.; Zagorin, p. 210; Gerard, *Autobiography*, p. 125.
37 Jardine, *Equivocation*, p. 16.
38 Edwards, *Fawkes*, p. 215; Holmes, *Resistance*, p. 198; see Nowak, *passim*.
39 S.T., II, p. 180.
40 Caraman, *Garnet*, p. 354.
41 Anstruther, *Vaux*, p. 341.

Chapter Sixteen: The Jesuits' Treason

1 Anstruther, *Vaux*, p. 345; C.S.P. Domestic, VIII, p. 292.
2 Edwards, *Tesimond*, p. 159 note.
3 Morris, *Gerard's Narrative*, p. 186.
4 Morris, *Gerard's Narrative*, p. 186; Waugh, pp. 21–2.
5 Anstruther, *Vaux*, p. 345; H.M.C. Salisbury, XVIII, p. 98; Waugh, p. 23.
6 Morris, *Gerard's Narrative*, pp. 188–90.
7 Edwards, *Tesimond*, p. 184.
8 Edwards, *Tesimond*, p. 184.
9 Caraman, *Garnet*, pp. 360–2.
10 Chamberlain, I, p. 219.
11 Caraman, *Garnet*, pp. 362–3.

12 C.S.P. Domestic, VIII, p. 291 note.

13 S.P. 14/216/241; Anstruther, *Vaux*, p. 344.

14 Anstruther, *Vaux*, pp. 345ff.; Caraman, *Garnet*, p. 367; see Gardiner, 'Garnet's Declarations', pp. 510–19.

15 Edwards, *Tesimond*, p. 191; H.M.C. Salisbury, XVIII, p. 98.

16 Caraman, *Garnet*, p. 386; Anstruther, *Vaux*, pp. 341, 357; H.M.C. Salisbury, XVIII, p. 108.

17 S.T., II, p. 243.

18 Gardiner, 'Garnet's Declarations', pp. 510–17.

19 Edwards, *Tesimond*, pp. 191–2.

20 Gardiner, 'Garnet's Declarations', p. 515; Holmes, 'Casuistry', p. 37; Caraman, *Garnet*, p. 376.

21 Gardiner, 'Garnet's Declarations', p. 514; but Fr Caraman accepted that the handwriting was Fr Garnet's own, *Garnet*, p. 376 note 4.

22 Gardiner, 'Garnet's Declarations', pp. 517–19.

23 Morris, *Gerard's Narrative*, p. 171.

24 S.P. 14/216/200; 201, Anstruther, *Vaux*, pp. 353–6.

25 Morris, *Gerard's Narrative*, p. 225.

26 S.T., II, pp. 217–355; Morris, *Gerard's Narrative*, pp. 226–64.

27 Anstruther, *Vaux*, p. 360; Wake, p. 40.

28 Caraman, *Garnet*, p. 391.

29 Caraman, *Garnet*, pp. 390–1.

30 Paul, pp. 248–50.

31 *Macbeth* (Muir), p. xxi.

32 Habington, p. 119; Humphreys, 'Wyntours', p. 74; Morris, *Gerard's Narrative*, p. 269.

33 Morris, *Gerard's Narrative*, p. 288.

34 Caraman, *Garnet*, p. 424; H.M.C. Salisbury, XVIII, pp. 95–6.

35 Caraman, *Garnet*, p. 429.

Chapter Seventeen: Farewells

1 Morris, *Gerard's Narrative*, p. 289.

2 Anstruther, *Vaux*, p. 368.

3 Morris, *Gerard's Narrative*, p. 290.

4 Morris, *Gerard's Narrative*, p. 290.

5 S.T., II, p. 355.

6 S.T., II, pp. 355–6.

7 Morris, *Gerard's Narrative*, pp. 292–3.

8 S.T., II, p. 356; Morris, *Gerard's Narrative*, p. 293.

9 Morris, *Gerard's Narrative*, pp. 293–4.
10 Morris, *Gerard's Narrative*, p. 295; S.T., II, p. 358.
11 Loomie, 'Toleration', p. 48; Gerard, *Autobiography*, p. 209.
12 Gerard, *Autobiography*, p. xvii.
13 Warnicke, pp. 170 and note 20, 182.
14 Anstruther, *Vaux*, p. 183.
15 Anstruther, *Vaux*, p. 184.
16 Morris, *Gerard's Narrative*, pp. 300–1; Caraman, *Garnet*, App. D, pp. 442–3 and note 1.
17 Caraman, *Years*, p. 12.
18 Anstruther, *Vaux*, p. 385.
19 Anstruther, *Vaux*, pp. 396, 453.
20 Peters, p. 385; Anstruther, *Vaux*, p. 476.
21 Gotch, *Old Halls*, p. 62; G.E.C. Banbury.
22 Baker, I, p. 245.
23 Finch, pp. 92–9.
24 Wake, p. 39 note 6.
25 Foley, IV, p. 136.
26 D.N.B. Kenelm Digby.
27 G.E.C. Monteagle; Hamilton, II, p. 37.
28 D.N.B. Ambrose Rookwood, 1664–96.
29 Goodman, I, pp. 118–22.
30 Southern, pp. 46, 83 note 3; Kerman, p. 49.
31 Nicholls, p. 77.
32 G.E.C. Monteagle.
33 Morris, *Gerard's Narrative*, pp. 27–8, 271; D.N.B. William Habington.
34 G.E.C. Salisbury; Croft, 'Cecil and Court', p. 140; H.M.C. Salisbury, XVIII, p. 535.
35 Nicholls, pp. 185, 165–6; Shirley, pp. 353, 340.
36 Shirley, p. 354.
37 Batho, 'Wizard Earl', pp. 344–7.
38 Rowse, *Cornwall*, p. 371; Peters, p. 74.
39 Bliss, p. 110; Loomie, 'Catholic Consort', p. 308.
40 H.M.C. Salisbury, XVIII, p. 178.

Chapter Eighteen: Satan's Policy?

1 Nicholls, p. 218.
2 Cressy, 'November', p. 72.
3 Milward, p. 62; *Macbeth*, Act II, scene iii; S.T., II, p. 164.

4 Nichols, I, pp. 38–9.

5 Haynes, *Plot*, App. I, p. 138.

6 Dekker, *Double P P*, prelude.

7 *Macbeth*, Act II, scene iii; *Macbeth* (Muir), pp. xvff.

8 *Macbeth*, Act V, scene v.

9 *Gager's Pyramis*, pp. 250ff.

10 Edwards, *Tesimond*, p. 139.

11 Lingard, VII, pp. 86–7 and note 1.

12 Clancy, 'Deposing Power', pp. 209ff.

13 Caraman, *Years*, p. 14; Anstruther, *Vaux*, p. 373.

14 Milton, IV, pp. 320–1.

15 C.S.P. Venetian, X, pp. 291–2; Edwards, *Fawkes*, p. 138.

16 H.M.C. Salisbury, XVIII, p. 508; Gerard, *What Plot?*, p. 430.

17 Goodman, I, pp. ix, 102.

18 Barlow, Preface.

19 S.T., II, p. 211.

20 Hazlitt, XI, p. 319.

21 L.J., IV, p. 369a; reference supplied by Mr D. L. Jones, Librarian, House of Lords.

22 C.J., XXX, p. 530; L.J., XIII, pp. 305b–306a; Cressy, 'November', p. 87, who however dates the search only to the 1690s; but see note 21 supra.

23 L.J., XIV, pp. 570a, 571b–572a.

24 Smith, *Westminster*, p. 44.

25 Paget, pp. 73–4; information to the author.

26 Cressy, 'November', p. 69.

27 See Nowak, *passim*; Andrewes, pp. 889–90.

28 Cressy, 'November', pp. 73ff.; Cressy, *Bonfires*, pp. 162ff.

29 Hutton, p. 212.

30 Shaw, pp. 15–18; Whitehill, p. 29; *Folklore*, p. 386.

31 Shaw, pp. 15–18; Billington, pp. 18–19; *Folklore*, p. 386.

32 Miller, p. 15; Blunt, pp. 730–1; Cressy, 'November', pp. 71–2; Keeling, p. 398; Colley, p. 21.

33 Swift, 'Fawkes in Exeter', p. 61.

34 Norman, p. 61.

35 Jardine, *Narrative*, p. 155.

36 See Quinault, 'Warwickshire Landowners'.

37 'Diary of Joan Courthope', unpub.

38 Lewes Bonfire Night Special, *Sussex Express*, 11 November 1994.

39 *The Night of the Fires*, 11 November 1994; local information to the author; *Folklore*, p. 386.

40 Gardiner, *England*, I, pp. 263–4.
41 Morris, *Gerard's Narrative*, p. 10 and note 4; Edwards, *Tesimond*, p. 214.
42 Nelson Mandela, *Long Walk to Freedom*, 1994, pp. 350–1.
43 Recalling Clarendon's final judgement on Oliver Cromwell: 'a brave bad man'; Clarendon, Edward Earl of, *History of the Rebellion ...*, p. 97, Oxford, 1969.

Reference Books

Details only of those books, documents, etc. cited in abbreviated form in the References; a full bibliography is impracticable for reasons of space. The place of publication is London unless otherwise stated.

Akrigg, G. P. V., *Jacobean Pageant*, 1962

Allen, Kenneth, *The Story of Gunpowder*, 1973

Allison, A. F., 'The Writings of Fr Henry Garnet, S.J. (1555–1606)', *Biographical Studies*, I, 1951

Andrewes, Lancelot, *XCVI Sermons*, 3rd edn, 1635

Anstruther, Godfrey, O.P., 'Powder Treason', *Blackfriars*, 33, 1952

Anstruther, Godfrey, O.P., *Vaux of Harrowden: a recusant family*, Newport, Mon., 1953

Ashton, Robert, ed., *James I by his Contemporaries*, 1969

Aveling, Dom. Hugh, O.S.B., 'The Catholic Recusants of the West Riding of Yorkshire, 1558–1790', *Proceedings of the Leeds Philosophical & Literary Society*, Leeds, X, 1963

Aveling, Dom. Hugh, O.S.B., 'The Marriages of Catholic Recusants', *Journal of Ecclesiastical History*, 14, 1963

Aveling, Dom. Hugh, O.S.B., *Post Reformation Catholicism in East Yorkshire 1558–1790*, York, 1960

Aveling, J. C. H., *The Handle and the Axe: the Catholic recusants in England from Reformation to Emancipation*, 1976

Baker, George, *History of Antiquities in the County of Northampton*, I, 1822

Barlow, Thomas, *The Gunpowder Treason...with Appendix of Several Papers written by Sir Everard Digby during his confinement*, 1679, reprinted 1850

Barroll, Leeds, 'The Court of the First Stuart Queen', in *The Mental World of the Jacobean Court*, ed. Linda L. Peck, Cambridge, 1991

Bassett, Bernard, S.J., *The English Jesuits from Campion to Martindale*, 1967

Batho, G. R., 'The Wizard Earl in the Tower 1605–1621', *History Today*, 6, 1956

Batho, G. R., *The Household Papers of Henry Percy, Ninth Earl of Northumberland (1564–1632)*, Camden Society, 3rd series, XCIII, 1962

Bellamy, John, *The Tudor Law of Treason: an introduction*, 1979

Billington, Ray Allen, *The Protestant Crusade, 1800–1860: a study of the origins of American nativism*, New York, 1938

Birch, Thomas, *An Historical View of Negotiations between the Courts of England, France and Brussels, 1592–1617*, 1749

(B.L.) British Library MSS

Bliss, W., 'Note on the Religious Belief of Anne of Denmark', *English Historical Review*, 4, 1889

Blunt, J. H., *The Annotated Book of Common Prayer*, new edn, 1888

Bodleian Library, Oxford

Bossy, John, 'Henri IV, the Appellants and the Jesuits', *Recusant History*, 8, 1965

Bossy, John, 'The Character of English Catholicism', in *Crisis in Europe 1560–1660*, ed. Trevor Aston, 1970

Bossy, John, 'The English Catholic Community. 1603–1605', in *The Reign of King James VI and I*, ed. A. G. R. Smith, 1973

Bossy, John, *Giordano Bruno and the Embassy Affair*, pbk, 1992

Boyle, Conall, *In the Footsteps of the Gunpowder Plotters: a journey through history in Middle England*, Meridian books, Oldbury, West Midlands, 1994

Bridges, John, *History of Northamptonshire*, 2 Vols, Oxford, 1791

Bruce, John, ed., *Correspondence of James VI with Sir Robert Cecil and others in England*, Camden Society, 1861

Bull, S., 'Furie of the Ordnance', unpublished thesis, University of Wales, 1988

Byrne, M. St Clare, *Elizabethan Life in Town and Country*, 8th revised edn, 1961

Camm, Dom. Bede, O.S.B., *Forgotten Shrines*, 1910

Caraman, Philip, ed., *The Other Face. Catholic life under Elizabeth I*, 1960

Caraman, Philip, *Henry Garnet 1555–1606 and the Gunpowder Plot*, 1964

Caraman, Philip, ed., *The Years of Siege: Catholic life from James I to Cromwell*, 1966

The Memoirs of Robert Carey, ed. F. H. Mares, Oxford, 1972

Carswell, Donald, ed., *Trial of Guy Fawkes and Others (The Gunpowder Plot)*, 1934

The Letters of John Chamberlain, ed. N. E. McClure, 2 Vols, Philadelphia, 1939

Chambers, M. C. E., *The Life of Mary Ward, 1585–1645*, 2 Vols, 1885

Charles-Edwards, T., *Saint Winefride and her Well: the historical background*, n.d.

(C.J.) *Journals of the House of Commons, 1547–1628*, 1803

Clancy, T., S.J., 'English Catholics and the Papal Disposing Power, 1570–1640', *Recusant History*, 6, 1961

Clancy, T. H., S.J., *Papist Pamphleteers*, Chicago, 1964

Clark, Sir George, 'Jacobean Northamptonshire, 1603–1625', *Northamptonshire Past and Present*, 2, 1958

The Diary of the Lady Anne Clifford, with an Introductory Note by V. Sackville-West, 1923

Coke, Edward, *The Third and Fourth Parts of the Institutes of the Laws of England...*, 1654

Colley, Linda, *Britons: Forging the nation, 1707–1837*, 1992

Collinson, Patrick, *The Elizabethan Puritan Movement*, 1967

Cooper, W. D., 'Further Particulars of Thomas Norton, and of State Proceedings in Matters of Religion in the Years 1581 and 1582', *Archaeologia*, 36, 1855

Coughton Court and the Throckmortons, National Trust, Norwich, 1993

'Diary of Joan Courthope 1886–1974', unpub., ed. Richard Rose

Cressy, David, *Bonfires and Bells. national memory and the Protestant calendar in Elizabethan and Stuart England*, 1989

Cressy, David, 'The Fifth of November Remembered', in *Myths of the English*, ed. Roy Porter, Oxford, 1992

Croft, Pauline, 'The Reputation of Robert Cecil: libels, political opinion and popular awareness in the early seventeenth century', *Transactions of the Royal Historical Society*, 6th Series, I, 1990

Croft, Pauline, 'Robert Cecil and the Early Jacobean Court', in *The Mental World of the Jacobean Court*, ed. Linda Levy Peck, Cambridge, 1991

Cruickshank, *Elizabeth's Army*, 2nd edn, Oxford, 1966

Reference Books

(C.S.P.) Calendar of State Papers, Domestic, in the reign of Elizabeth, 1601–1603, 1870

(C.S.P.) Calendar of State Papers, Domestic, 1603–1610, VIII, 1857

(C.S.P.) Calendar of State Papers, Spanish, IV, 1899

(C.S.P.) Calendar of State Papers, Venetian, X, 1900

Cuddy, Neil, 'The Revival of the Entourage: the bedchamber of James I, 1603–1625', in *The English Court: from the Wars of the Roses to the Civil War*, ed. David Starkey, 1987

Cuvelier, Joseph, 'Les Préliminaires du traité de Londres (29 âout 1604)', *Revue Belge de Philologie et d'Histoire*, 2, 1923, Bruxelles

David, Rev. Christopher, *St Winefride's Well: a history and guide. An illustrated description*, reprint, 1993

Dekker, Thomas, *The Double P P. A Papist in Armes. Bearing Ten severall Sheilds Encountred by the Protestant. At Ten severall Weapons. A Iesuite Marching before them*, 1606

Dekker, Thomas, *The Non-Dramatic Works*, ed. A. B. Crosart, 4 Vols, 1884

Devlin, Christopher, *Hamlet's Divinity*, 1963

Devlin, Christopher, *The Life of Robert Southwell: poet and martyr*, 1967

Dickens, A. G., 'The First Stages of Romanist Recusancy in Yorkshire, 1560–1590', *Yorkshire Archaeological Journal*, 35, 1943

Dickens, A. G., 'The Extent and Character of Recusancy in Yorkshire, 1604', *Yorkshire Archaeological Journal*, 37, 1945

(D.N.B.) Dictionary of National Biography

Dodd, A. H., 'The Spanish Treason, the Gunpowder Plot, and the Catholic Refugees', *English Historical Review*, 53, 1938

Doleman, R., *A Conference about the Next Succession to the Crowne of Ingland 1594*, ed. D. M. Rogers, Menston, Yorks., 1972

Duffy, Eamon, *The Stripping of the Altars: traditional religion in England c. 1400–c. 1580*, 1992

Dures, Alan, *English Catholicism 1558–1642: community and change*, 1983

Eastward Ho!, by Ben Jonson, George Chapman and John Marston, ed. C. G. Peter, 1973

Edwards, Francis, S.J., *Guy Fawkes: the real story of the Gunpowder Plot?*, 1969

Edwards, Francis, S.J., ed., *The Gunpowder Plot: the narrative of Oswald Tesimond alias Greenway*, trans. from the Italian of the Stonyhurst Manuscript, edited and annotated, 1973

Edwards, Francis, S.J., *The Jesuits in England: from 1580 to the present day*, 1985

Edwards, Francis, S.J., 'Still Investigating Gunpowder Plot', *Recusant History*, 21, 1993

Elliott, J. H., *Imperial Spain, 1469–1716*, 1969

Elton, G. R., *The Practice of History*, Sydney, 1967

Fea, Allan, *Secret Chambers and Hiding-Places*, 3rd & revised edn, 1908

Finch, Mary E., *The Wealth of Five Northamptonshire Families 1540–1640*, Oxford, 1956

Fisher, H. A. L., *Frederick William Maitland: a biographical sketch*, Cambridge, 1910

Foley, Henry, S.J., *Records of the English Province of the Society of Jesus*, 7 Vols, 1st Series, 1877–83

The Folklore of American Holidays, ed. Hennig Cohen and Tristram Potter Coffin, 2nd edn, Detroit, n.d.

Francis, Rev. P. H., *The Origins and Developments of Fire Arms and Gunpowder*, Bradford, 1961

William Gager's Pyramis, ed. C. F. Tucker Brooke, *Transactions of the Connecticut Academy of Arts and Sciences*, 32, 1936, New Haven, Conn.

Gardiner, S. R., *History of England, 1603–1607*, I, 1883

Gardiner, S. R., 'Two Declarations of Garnet relating to the Gunpowder Plot', *English Historical Review*, III, 1888

Gardiner, S. R., *What Gunpowder Plot Was*, 1897

[Garnet, Henry], 'Treatise of Equivocation', MS. Laud Misc. 655, Bodleian Library

Gearty, Conor, *Terror*, 1991

(G.E.C.) *The Complete Peerage … Extant Extinct or Dormant*, by G. E. C., 6 Vols, reprint, Gloucester, 1982

Gerard, John, *The Autobiography of an Elizabethan*, trans. from the Latin by Philip Caraman, with an introduction by Graham Greene, 1951

Gerard, John, 'Traditional History and the Spanish Treason of 1601–1603', *The Month*, 87, 1896

Gerard, John, *The Gunpowder Plot and the Gunpowder Plotters, in reply to Professor Gardiner*, 1897

Gerard, John, S.J., *What was the Gunpowder Plot? The traditional story tested by original evidence*, 1897

Gibbon, Edward, *The History of the Decline and Fall of the Roman Empire*, ed. J. B. Bury, 7 Vols, 8th edn, 1923

Goodman, Dr Godfrey, *The Court of King James the First*, 2 Vols, 1839

Gotch, J. Alfred, *A complete account of the buildings erected in Northamptonshire by Sir Thomas Tresham*, 1883

Gotch, J. Alfred, *Old Halls and Manor Houses of Northamptonshire*, 1936

Grosvenor, Ian D., 'Catholics and Politics: the Worcester election of 1604', *Recusant History*, 14, 1977–80

Habington, Thomas, *A Survey of Worcestershire*, Worcestershire Historical Society, ed. John Amphlet of Cleat, Vol. II, Pt I, Oxford, 1896

Haigh, Christopher, ed., *The Reign of Elizabeth I*, 1984

Haigh, Christopher, *English Reformations*, Oxford, 1993

Hale, John, *The Civilization of Europe in the Renaissance*, 1993

Hales, J. W., 'Round about Stratford in 1605', *Notes and Essays*, 1884

Hamilton, Dom. Adam, O.S.B., ed., *The Chronicle of the English Augustinian Canonesses Regular of the Lateran, at St Monica's in Louvain*, 2 Vols, 1904–6

Handover, P. M., *Arbella Stuart: royal lady of Hardwick and cousin to King James*, 1957

Handover, P. M., *The Second Cecil: the rise to power 1563–1604 of Sir Robert Cecil, later first Earl of Salisbury*, 1959

Hanlon, Sr. Joseph Damian, 'These Be But Women', in *From the Renaissance to the Counter Reformation: essays in honour of Garrett Mattingly*, ed. C. H. Carter, 1966

Harrison, G. B., *A Last Elizabethan Journal: being a record of those things most talked of during the years 1599–1603*, 1933

Harrison, G. B., *A Jacobean Journal: being a record of those things most talked of during the years 1603–1606*, 1941

Hatfield MSS, Hatfield House, Herts

Haynes, Alan, *Robert Cecil, Earl of Salisbury, 1563–1612: servant of two sovereigns*, 1989

Haynes, Alan, *The Gunpowder Plot*, Stroud, Glos., 1994

The Collected Works of William Hazlitt, ed. A. R. Walter and A. Glover, 11, 1904

Hicks, L., S.J., 'Sir Robert Cecil, Father Persons and the Succession. 1600–1601', *Archivum Historicum Societatis Iesu*, 24, 1955

Hicks, L., S.J., 'Father Robert Persons S.J. and *The Book of Succession*', *Recusant History*, 4, 1957

Hicks, L., S.J., 'The Embassy of Sir Anthony Standen in 1603', *Recusant History*, 5, 1959

(H.M.C.) Historical Manuscripts Commission, Report on the Manuscripts of Lord Montagu of Beaulieu, 1900

(H.M.C.) Historical Manuscripts Commission, Calendar of the Manuscripts of the Most Honourable the Marquess of Salisbury, Vols XI–XVIII, 1906–40

Hogrefe, Pearl, *Tudor Women: commoners and queens*, Ames, Iowa, 1975

Holmes, P., 'Elizabethan Casuistry', *Catholic Record Society*, 67, 1981

Holmes, Peter, *Resistance and Compromise: the political thought of Elizabethan Catholics*, Cambridge, 1982

Gerard Manley Hopkins, ed. Catherine Phillips, Oxford, 1986

Hotson, Leslie, *I, William Shakespeare*, 1937

Humphreys, John, 'The Wyntours of Huddington and the Gunpowder Plot', *Transactions of the Birmingham and Midlands Institute*, 30, 1904

Humphreys, John, 'The Habingtons of Hindlip and the Gunpowder Plot', *Transactions of the Birmingham and Midlands Institute*, 31, 1905

Hurstfield, Joel, 'Robert Cecil Earl of Salisbury: minister of Elizabeth and James I', *History Today*, 7, 1957

Hurstfield, Joel, 'The Succession Struggle in late Elizabethan England', in *Elizabethan Government and Society: Essays presented to Sir John Neale*, ed. S. T. Bindoff, J. Hurstfield and C. H. Williams, 1961

Hurstfield, Joel, *Freedom, Corruption and Government in Elizabethan England*, 1973

Hutton, Ronald, *The Rise and Fall of Merry England 1400–1700*, Oxford, 1994

Jardine, David, ed., *Criminal Trials, II: The Gunpowder Plot*, 1835

Jardine, David, *A Reading on the Use of Torture in the Criminal Law of England previously to the Commonwealth*, 1837

Jardine, David, 'Observations on the historical evidence supporting the Implication of Lord Mounteagle as a Conspirator in the Gunpowder Treason', *Archaeologia*, XXIX, 1844

Jardine, David, 'Remarks upon Letters of Thomas Winter and Lord Mounteagle, lately discovered by John Bruce, Esq., F.S.A.', *Archaeologia*, XXIX, 1844

Jardine, David, ed., *A Treatise of Equivocation*, 1851

Jardine, David, *A Narrative of the Gunpowder Plot*, 1857

Johnson, Paul, *Elizabeth I: a study in power and intellect*, pbk, 1988

Jones, Mary Whitmore, *The Gunpowder Plot and Life of Robert Catesby also an account of Chastleton House*, 1909

Jordan, W. K., *The Development of Religious Toleration in England: from the accession of James I to the convention of the Long Parliament (1603–1640)*, II, 1936

Keeling, William D. D., *Liturgicae Britannicae*, 1842

Kerman, Joseph, *The Masses and Motets of William Byrd*, 1981

King James' History of the Gunpowder Plot, State Trials, II, 1809

King Lear, The Arden Shakespeare, ed. Kenneth Muir, reprinted with corrections, 1972

(*King's Book*) *His Majesties Speach in this Last Session of Parliament... Together with a discourse of the maner of the discouery of the late intended Treason, ioyned with an Examination of some of the prisoners*, 1605

The Kings Majesties Speech ... to the Lords ... On Munday the 19 day of March 1603, 1604

Klingenstein, L., *The Great Infanta: Isabel, Sovereign of the Netherlands*, 1910

Laffleur De Kermaingant, P., *Mission de Christophe de Harlay Comte de Beaumont (1602–1605)*, Paris, 2 Vols, 1895

Larkin, James F., and Hughes, Paul L., eds, *Stuart Royal Proclamations*, 2 Vols, Oxford, 1973–80

The Lawes Resolutions of Woman's Rights, or the Lawes Provisions for Women, 1632

Leatherbarrow, J. S., *The Lancashire Elizabethan Recusants*, Chetham Society, New Series, 110, Manchester, 1947

Lee, Maurice, Jr, *James I and Henri VI: an essay in English foreign policy, 1603–1610*, Urbana, Ill., 1970

Lewalski, Barbara K., 'Lucy, Countess of Bedford: images of a Jacobean courtier and patroness', in *Politics of Discourse*, ed. Kevin Sharpe and Steven N. Zwicker, Berkeley, Calif., 1987

Lingard, John, *The History of England*, VII, 5th edn, 1849

(L.J.) *Journal of the House of Lords*, IV, XIV

Longley, Katharine M., 'Three Sites in the City of York', *Recusant History*, 12, 1973

Longueville, Thomas, *The Life of a Conspirator*, 1895

Loomie, Albert J., S.J., *The Spanish Elizabethans: exiles at the Court of Philip II*, 1963

Loomie, Albert J., S.J., 'Toleration and Diplomacy: the religious issue in Anglo-Spanish relations, 1603–1605', *Transactions of the American Philosophical Society*, Philadelphia, New series, 53, Pt 6, 1963

Loomie, Albert J., S.J., 'Philip III and the Stuart Succession in England, 1600–1603', *Revue Belge de Philologie et d'Histoire*, 43, 1965, Bruxelles

Loomie, Albert J., S.J., *Guy Fawkes in Spain: the 'Spanish Treason' in Spanish documents*, *Bulletin of the Institute of Historical Research*, Special Supplement no. 9, November 1971

Loomie, Albert J., S.J., 'King James I's Catholic Consort', *Huntington Library Quarterly*, 34, 1971

Loomie, Albert J., S.J., *Spain and the Jacobean Catholics*, I: *1603–1612*, Catholic Record Society, 1973

Luna, B. N. De, *Jonson's Romish Plot: a study of Catiline and its historical context*, Oxford, 1967

Macbeth, The Arden Shakespeare, ed. Kenneth Muir, reprinted with new introduction, 1992

MacCaffrey, Wallace, *Elizabeth I*, 1993

McIlwain, C. H., ed., *The Political Works of James I*, Cambridge, Mass., 1918

Mackie, J. D., 'The Secret Diplomacy of King James VI in Italy prior to his Accession to the English Throne', *Scottish Historical Review*, 21, 1923–4

Magee, Brian, *The English Recusants: a study of the post-Reformation Catholic survival and the operation of the recusancy laws*, with an introduction by Hilaire Belloc, 1938

Malloch, A. E., 'Father Henry Garnet's Treatise of Equivocation', *Recusant History*, 15, 1981

Diary of John Manningham, ed. John Bruce, Camden Society, 1868

Mathew, David, *Catholicism in England: the portrait of a minority: its culture and tradition*, 2nd revised edn, 1948

Mathew, David, *James I*, 1967

Miller, John, *Religion in the Popular Prints, 1600–1832*, Cambridge, 1986

Complete Prose Works of John Milton, IV, 1650–1655, Pt 1, New Haven, Conn., 1966

Milward, Peter, *Shakespeare's Religious Background*, 1973

Morris, John, S.J., *The Condition of Catholics under James I: Father Gerard's Narrative of the Gunpowder Plot*, 2nd edn, 1872

Morris, John, S.J., *The troubles of our Catholic forefathers*, First series, 1872

Munden, R. C., 'James I and "the Growth of Mutual Distrust": King, Commons and reform, 1603–1604', in *Faction and Parliament: essays in early Stuart History*, ed. Kevin Sharpe, Oxford, 1978

Nash, T. R., 'Copy of the original Death-Warrant of Humphrey Littleton', *Archaeologia*, 15, 1803

Nash, Thomas, *The History and Antiquities of Worcestershire*, 2 Vols, 1781

Neale, J. E., 'The Sayings of Queen Elizabeth', *History*, New Series, 10, 1925

Neale, J. E. *Elizabeth I and her Parliaments 1559–1581*, I, 1953

Neale, J. E. *Elizabeth I and her Parliaments 1584–1601*, II, 1957

(Nicholls) Nicholls, Mark, *Investigating Gunpowder Plot*, 1991

Nicholls, Mark, 'Sir Walter Ralegh's Treason: a prosecution document', *English Historical Review*, CX, 1995

Nicholls, Mark, 'Treason's Reward: the punishment of conspirators in the Bye Plot of 1603', *Historical Journal*, 38, 1995

Nichols, John, *The Progresses ... of King James the First*, 4 Vols, 1828

The Night of the Fires, compiled and produced by David Perry, Perryscope Productions, BBC Radio 3, 11 November 1994

Norman, E. R., *Anti-Catholicism in Victorian England*, 1968

Nowak, T. S., '"Remember, Remember the Fifth of November": Anglocentrism and anti-Catholicism in the English Gunpowder sermons, 1605–1651', Ph.D. thesis, State University of New York at Stony Brook, 1992

O'Halloran, Simon, *Bonfires in Lewes: a history of the celebrations on November the Fifth*, privately printed, 1967

Oman, Carola, *Elizabeth of Bohemia*, revised edn, 1964

Paget, Julian, *The Yeomen of the Guard: five hundred years of service. 1485–1985*, Poole, Dorset, 1984

Parker, Geoffrey, *The Dutch Revolt*, 1979

Parker, Geoffrey, *Europe in Crisis, 1598–1648*, Brighton, Sussex, 1980

Parnell, Geoffrey, *Book of the Tower of London*, English Heritage, 1993

Paul, H. N., *The Royal Play of Macbeth*, New York, 1950

Peck, Linda Levy, *Northampton: patronage and policy at the court of James I*, 1982

Peck, Linda Levy, *Court Patronage and Corruption in Early Stuart England*, Boston, Mass., 1990

Peck, Linda Levy, ed., *The Mental World of the Jacobean Court*, Cambridge, 1991

Peters, Henriette, *Mary Ward: a world in contemplation*, trans. Helen Butterworth, Leominster, Herefordshire, 1994

Pollen, J. H., S.J., 'The Accession of King James I', *The Month*, 101, 1903

Pollen, J. H., S.J., *The Institution of the Archpriest Blackwell*, 1916

Porter, Roy, *London. A social history*, 1994

(P.R.O.) Public Record Office, London

Quinault, Roland, 'Warwickshire Landowners and Parliamentary Politics 1841–1923', unpublished D.Phil. thesis, Oxford University, 1975

(R.C.H.) Royal Commission on Historical Monuments (England), London, V (East London), 1930

Read, Conyers, 'William Cecil and Elizabethan Public Relations', in *Elizabethan Government and Society: essays presented to Sir John Neale*, ed. S. T. Bindoff, J. Hurstfield and C. H. Williams, 1961

Ridley, Jasper, *Elizabeth I*, 1987

Robinson, John Martin, *The Dukes of Norfolk, A Quincentenniel History*, Oxford, 1982

Rodger, N. A. M., 'Ordnance Records and the Gunpowder Plot', *Bulletin of the Institute of Historical Research*, 53, 1980

Rodríguez-Villa, Antonio, ed., *Correspondencia de la Infanta Archiduquesa Doña Isabel Clara Eugenia de Austria con el Duque de Lerma y otros personajes*, Madrid, 1906

Rose, Elliot, *Cases of Conscience: alternatives open to recusants and Puritans under Elizabeth I and James I*, Cambridge, 1975

Rowlands, Marie B., 'Recusant Women 1560–1640', in *Women in English Society 1500–1800*, ed. Mary Prior, 1985

Rowse, A. L., *Tudor Cornwall: portrait of a society*, 1941

Rowse, A. L., *Raleigh and the Throckmortons*, 1962

Rowse, A. L., *Simon Forman: sex and society in Shakespeare's age*, 1974

Salgādo, Carmini, *The Elizabethan Underworld*, Stroud, Glos., 1992

Scarisbrick, J. J., *The Jesuits and the Catholic Reformation*, 1988

Seton, Walter W., 'The Early Years of Henry Frederick, Prince of Wales, and Charles, Duke of Albany (Charles I)', *Scottish Historical Review*, 13, 1915–16

Shakespeare Birthplace Trust, Shakespeare Centre, Stratford-upon-Avon

Shaw, Peter, *American Patriots and the Rituals of Revolution*, Cambridge, Mass., 1981

Shirley, John W., *Thomas Harriot: a biography*, Oxford, 1983

Simons, Eric N., *The Devil of the Vault*, 1963

Skinner, Quentin, *The Foundations of Modern Political Thought: The Age of Reformation*, Cambridge, 1978

Smith, Alan G. R., ed., *The Reign of James VI and I*, 1973

Smith, John Thomas, *Antiquities of Westminster; the Old Palace; St. Stephen's Chapel, (now the House of Commons) etc. etc.*, 1807

Somers, John, Baron, *A collection of scarce and valuable Tracts...*, 2nd revised edn, 13 Vols, 1809–15

Somerset, Anne, *Elizabeth I*, 1991

Southern A. C., ed., *The Elizabethan Recusant House, comprising The Life of the Lady Magdalen Viscountess Montague (1538–1608)*, 1954

The Poetical Works of the Rev. Robert Southwell, ed. William B. Turnbull, 1856

(S.P.) State Papers, Public Record Office, London

Spink, H. H., *The Gunpowder Plot and Lord Mounteagle's Letter*, 1902

Squiers, Granville, *Secret Hiding Places*, 1933

(S.T.) *State Trials, Cobbett's Complete Collection of…From the Earliest Period to the Present Time*, II, 1603–1627, 1809

Stafford, H. G., *James VI of Scotland and the Throne of England*, New York, 1940

Stevenson, Joseph, S.J., 'Anne of Denmark, Queen of Great Britain', *The Month*, 37, 1879

Stow, John, *Annales, or, A Generall Chronicle of England, Begun by John Stow. Continued by Edmund Howes*, 1631

Strong, Roy, *Henry, Prince of Wales and England's Lost Renaissance*, 1986

Sumner, Ann, ed., *Death, Passion and Politics*, Dulwich Picture Gallery, 1995.

Swift, Roger, 'Guy Fawkes Celebrations in Victorian Exeter', *History Today*, 31, 1981

Tierney, Rev. M. A., ed., *Dodd's Church History of England with Notes, Additions and a continuation*, 3 & 4, 1840–1

Torture and Punishment (Treasures of the Tower), H.M.S.O., 1973

Toyne, S. M., 'Guy Fawkes and the Powder Plot', *History Today*, I, 1951

Trimble, W. R., *The Catholic Laity in Elizabethan England*, Cambridge, Mass., 1964

Vaux, Laurence, *A Catechisme or Christian Doctrine*, with memoir by T. Law, Chetham Society, New Series, 4, 1885

(V.C.H.) Victoria County History, Worcestershire, III, 1913

Vetusta Monumenta, V, 1835

Wake, Joan, 'The Death of Francis Tresham', *Northamptonshire Past and Present*, 2, 1954

Walsham, Alexandra, *Church Papists: Catholicism, conformity and confessional polemic in early modern England*, Woodbridge, Suffolk, 1993

Ward, A. W., 'Review of W. Plenkers' "Was Frederick II's daughter Anne, Queen of Great Britain, a convert to Catholicism?"', *English Historical Review*, 2, 1888

Warner, G. F., 'James VI and Rome', *English Historical Review*, XX, 1905

Warnicke, Retha M., *Women of the English Renaissance and Reformation*, 1983

Waugh, Margaret, *Blessed Nicholas Owen: Jesuit Brother and maker of hiding holes*, 1959

Webb, William K. L., 'The Phantom Conspiracy', unpublished MS, Jesuit (Farm Street) Archives, London

Weller, Ralph B., 'Some Aspects of the Life of Richard Haydocke, Physician, Engraver, Painter and Translator (1569–?1642)', *The Hatcher Review*, 2, 1985

Weston, William, *Autobiography of an Elizabethan*, trans. from the Latin by Philip Caraman. With a foreword by Evelyn Waugh, 1955

Wharam, Alan, *Treason: famous English treason trials*, Stroud, Glos., 1995

Whitehill, W. M., *Boston: a topographical history*, Cambridge, Mass., 1959

Wiener, Carol Z., 'The Beleaguered Isle: a study of Elizabethan and early Jacobean anti-Catholicism', *Past and Present*, 51, 1971

The Journal of Sir Roger Wilbraham, ed. H. S. Scott, Camden Society, 10, 1902

Wilkinson, Paul, *Terrorism and the Liberal State*, New York, 1979

Williams, E. C., *Anne of Denmark*, 1970

Williams, Neville, *Elizabeth Queen of England*, 1967

Williamson, Hugh Ross, *The Gunpowder Plot*, 1951

Wills, Gary, *Witches and Jesuits: Shakespeare's Macbeth*, New York, 1995

Willson, D. H., *King James VI and I*, 1962 edn

Wood, Anthony à, *Athenae Oxonienses*, 1691

Wormald, Jenny, 'James VI and I: two Kings or one?' *History*, LXVIII, 1983

Wormald, Jenny, 'Gunpowder, Treason and Scots', *Journal of British Studies*, XXIV, Chicago, 1985

Zagorin, Perez, *Ways of Lying: dissimulation, persecution, and conformity in early modern Europe*, Cambridge, Mass., 1990

Index